Hans-Peter Kolb

Analysis of Being-There in Psychotherapy

Declarations of Love or True and Immediate Experience of Love?

Hans-Peter Kolb

Analysis of Being-There in Psychotherapy

Declarations of Love or True and Immediate Experience of Love?

Copyright © 2018 Hans-Peter Kolb
2018 amended version

All rights reserved.

ISBN: 9781980958178
Imprint: Independently published

Table of Contents

Preface

After I have approached the topic of the analysis of being-there and of the development of our capacity to love from a more philosophical perspective in earlier works, now, I want to consider the whole issue from a psychotherapeutic point of view. Which practical meaning is hidden in the analysis of being-there, pursued by me, for the psychotherapeutic treatment of patients, and how and by what in the therapeutic situation can the capacity for love be fostered in both, patient and therapist, and develop further on and on?

I came up with the idea of taking the expression "declarations of love" in the subtitle, because of its double meaning: on the one hand, I want to declare resp. to explain, how one's own capacity to love and that one of other ones can be fostered in one's particular development, on the other hand, I see a declaration of love for all human beings in the idea that each human being can develop his or her own capacity to love further on and on and faces up to this issue (he or she cannot help it), i.e. they are worth to be loved due to the mere fact that they are meant for loving themselves and others more and more, even if they do not do this by all means. However, declarations of love can be untrue, and if you explain something, it does not immediately reach the other one, it is mediated by speech and therefore without effect first and foremost. Only if something is experienced immediately, it is real for somebody in concern, and for that he or she must not only be receptive, but must become active, in this sense become a subject, actively submitting to certain processes (Latin subiectum = submitted) resp. risking being exposed. This has immediate effects and consequences for the psychotherapeutic situation.

At first, I sketchily shall describe the development of my own philosophical thinking regarding the analysis of our being-there, thereupon state the anthropology developed by my analysis, then include more and more psychological aspects, this lead-ing to a psychological theory of psychic disturbances, which I want to take appropriate psychotherapeutic action from. As indicated in the first paragraph of this preface, I always take a psychother-apeutic treatment as a mutual process, which in an ideal situation leads to a further development of their capacity to love for all in-volved.

After completion of this work, I have asked myself, how come that only now I have put the issue of psychotherapy at the heart of my analyses, although my main job is not being a philos-opher, but a psychotherapist. The only explanation I can give, is that the way of knowledge always leads from far off to ourselves, like Heidegger says that ontically we are the nearest, but ontolog-ically the farthest for ourselves. I first tried to get enough clarity philosophically, before I turned to my true area of activity, to psy-chotherapy.

1. The Development of My Analytic Thinking of Being-There

The decisive factor certainly was the reading of Heidegger (Heidegger, 2006a), who indeed established the modern analysis of being-there and chose the issue of death as main emphasis of that, to confront us with the denial of this topic in our culture. When he warned us of an overemphasizing of technics again and again, then I interpret this as a warning that otherwise we get punished like Sisyphos, who outfoxed Thanatos, the Greek god of death, and captivated him: again and again, Sisyphos had to roll up a very heavy stone to the top of a high mountain, and at the highest point the stone fell down the mountain. With us already today, there is a certain obsession to do everything better, faster, higher, farther etc. "To subdue the earth" you can interpret in another way, too, instead of recklessly exploiting it and denying evanescence and death.

By chance then, I came up with the Japanese philosophers of the Kyôto-school. They compared Heidegger's "truth of intrinsicality" with the "truth of Zen-Buddhism", the absolute nothingness. In Buddhism it is about overcoming all opposites, so that vanishing of space, i.e. Nirvana (non-spatial truth), arises and there is absolutely nothing concerning space. In contrast, our idea of redemption only knows timelessness in the eternity, where there still is some space, e.g. the obviously spatial separation of heaven (timeless intrinsicality) and hell (temporal persistent decayed state, to use Heidegger's way of expression).

Nishida, one of the founders of the Kyôto-school, takes up a problem of identity mediated by time, how we can remain the same while continuously changing (Nishida, 2011). On the other hand, Tanabe, the other founder of the Kyôto-school criticizes Nishida that he can overcome opposites, especially the one between the general of the joint being together and the individual being, only then, when he includes the action, which is the only thing that can bring about some turnaround (Tanabe, 2011). Therefore, Tanabe considers our being-there as some special being, as species, too. By this, he points up that between the three modes of the individuum, the genus (joint being together), and the species, there is an absolute dialectical conveyance, i.e. each one mediates between the two others, and these together convey the one (ibidem), so that no mode can be preferred.

Before I finally framed my approach of an analysis of being-there for the first time, I busied myself with the American philosopher Stanley Cavell resp. with his main work "The Claim of Reason" (Cavell, 1979). The interesting thing with Cavell is that he studied psychology as well as philosophy, and before that he had to decide, if he wanted to become a jazz-pianist or to study. On the one hand, this reading familiarized me with Wittgenstein, whom Cavell was concerned with extensively, on the other hand, I was fascinated by his interpretations of Shakespeare as a creative approach to philosophical and psychological questions, which deal with the relationship of body, mind, and psyche.

1.1. Heidegger

My analytical considerations about being-there essentially are shaped by Heidegger. The first contact with his philosophy I got in autumn of 2010 in Switzerland in Isenthal, Kanton Uri during a further training concerning the seminaries of Zollikon, Heidegger had given together with the Swiss psychiatrist Medard Boss (Heidegger, 2006b). Probably I felt in a similar way like the former listeners at those times in Zollikon. I had some difficulties to understand, which Heidegger basically was after and what he wanted to convey, but then I had tasted blood and wanted to delve into his thinking. So, I bought "Sein und Zeit" (translated "Being and Time" (Heidegger, 2006a)) and started to work through it and to write down my thoughts about it (Kolb, 2011) by additionally reading a book edited by Thomas Rentsch about "Sein und Zeit" (Rentsch, 2007).

A takeaway from there is that I interpreted Heidegger's "intrinsic sensational understanding for-the-sake-of-which"[1] or first the for-the-sake-of-which as perfect love, and altogether

---

[1] „das eigentliche befindliche Verstehen des Worumwillens"

Heidegger´s understanding as striving after intrinsic and immediate understanding of one´s own and other one´s for-the-sake-of-which, which for me is an instruction for perfect other- and self-love, how to have a direct experience of love. Like Heidegger, I am not about a metaphysical definition, but about an anti-metaphysical directive to be able to have an experience of the phenomenon in concern – Heidegger uses to call this "to point up" and borrows a protreptic (encouraging/advising) speech, which his listeners at Zollikon as well as myself in Isenthal did not understand at first. Heidegger points up for example that our self is phenomenally contained in our concern (German "Sorge"), and therefore you can experience it only in practical life. By this Heidegger emphasizes the mode of being-there of species the same way Tanabe does (Tanabe, 2011).

One important point of criticism of Heidegger I found in the &&61 – 66: I could show here that the timeliness is only a necessary, but not a sufficient condition to provide an adequate and thus complete frame to analyze the being/Sein of being-there. The sense of being, according to Heidegger´s definition the frame, which being gets intelligible in, is not only the timeliness, but also the spatiality. The combination I called processuality, which owns as a fourth ecstasy besides those of timeliness (I call them origin, future and arrival, in German "Herkunft, Zukunft und Ankunft", where the suffix "kunft" means "has come": that, what has come from the origin, that, where we shall come to in the future, and that, where we have come to and arrived) the ecstasy of information in addition (I call it in German "Auskunft", that, what has come out, if we have got a good outcome with others, who therefore give us good information). This coincides with the fact that we can understand our being-there not only by the where-from, the where-to resp. what-for, and the just-whereof, but necessarily also by the exchange and a good outcome with others when discussing our practical acting and the information contained in this about the where-from, the where-to, and the whereof. As a picture I imagine this frame that way: the basic line of the frame describes the ecstasy of information, the line on the left side represents the origin, the one on the right side the future, and both side lines support together the upper line, which corresponds to the arrival.

While working through "Sein und Zeit" I conceived the following supplements and nuancing thoughts: Heidegger's concern ("Sorge") I differentiated into seizedness and expectation, where later it struck me that there is a parallel to Aristotle, who distinguishes between desire (orexis) and thinking (Aristoteles, 1985) and looks at human beings as beings, where thinking desire and desiring thinking collide. In his lectures on Aristotle Heidegger is said to have translated orexis by concern (Rentsch, 2007, p. 40). What Heidegger calls ruinousness ("Verfallenheit"), I refer to as a lack of examination of illusion and disappointments, so that in my diction the essence of being-there is seizedness, expectation, and illusion, whereby the dealing with illusion and with the resulting sensation of disappointment is the critical moment, if the being-there turns away from oneself and decays or does not.

Further, I interpreted the capability-to-be-guilty as deficiency, what the being-there assumes responsibility for not only in such a way (1) that one conceptualizes oneself into the future prepared for anxiety, but also (2) that one is ready to deal with the anger of other ones about one's deficiencies in a regretting manner and with one's own anger about it pardonably resp. mercifully, and by this more and more understands one's own thrownness, when sensational regretting, and the thrownness of other ones by not taking personally evil anything if possible, and (3) that one is ready to accept the suffering of other ones and of oneself in such a way that one develops abilities to make amends as appropriate and thus to change one's sense and direction in terms of metanoia or penance. Essentially contained in penance is the promise to develop one's ability to love. Generally, I did not only analyze anxiety, but also other basic sensations like delight, anger, and suffering in its "intrinsic"[2] and "non-intrinsic" form. To consider something from different "equiprimordial" sides, even

---

[2] What Heidegger calls "intrinsic", e.g. the anxiety, is in my terms a sensation or sensational state of mind associated with the mode of the individual seen from the angle of the psychic-motivational aspect, while "non-intrinsic" denotes a specific feeling, e.g. the fear, if it is about decisions seen from the angle of the mindful-idealistic aspect.

Heidegger himself suggests, when pointing to the frequent disregard of this phenomenon of equiprimordiality (Heidegger, 2006a, S. 131). The willingness to accept one´s anxiety in the actual situation in order preferably not to become factually guilty in the future, the regret about, where actual suffering comes from resp. has its origin, and penance (as defined above) as a new determined orientation in the present situation, where one has arrived, these are equiprimordial and constitute as different moments the phenomenon of being-guilty.

1.2. The Kyôto-School

On the search for more authors setting one´s wits to Heidegger, I came across a book about the Kyôto-school (Ohashi, 2011), in which one chapter dealt with the nothing by Heidegger. In Japan, a radical thinking about death and the nothingness of the human being-there had developed because of the frequent natural catastrophes, much more radical than in our culture, so that the absolute nothing (zettai mu) became a godlike position as the primal ground of being and nothing. Soon, I interpreted this as an equivalent to my concept of perfect love, which, as a utopia, is absolute nothing, too, because it can never be. I have written down these thoughts as well (Kolb, 2012a).

In the first chapter of Ohashi´s book Nishida is concerned with the identity problem given by time, how we can remain the same, although we always change by time. By this, he comes across the answer that, for the solution of this problem, we must overcome the five opposites active-passive, objective-subjective, continuous-discontinuous, linear-circular, and spatial-temporal. Thereby, it occurred to me that this can be brought into line with the development of the self as represented by Fonagy et al. (Fonagy, Gergely, Jurist, & Target, 2004). Later, when I dealt with the Nicomachean Ethics (Aristoteles, 1985), I also saw in this the development of the five dianoetic virtues reason, science, craftsmanship, prudence, and wisdom, as well as our so called five senses, how we use them by language from their emotional meaning. The five ways of learning then are by insight, rear view/regard, foresight/precaution, prospect, and circumspect[3].

If we acquire a *taste* for something, we *delight*, become *active* and understand as a *physical self* with *insight* and *reason* basic relationships and principles; depending on whether we can *smell* (in the sense of like) someone or not, it stinks, we get *angry* or find it *disgusting* as a *subject* confronted with an *object*, and try as a *social self* with *regard* for other ones and for ourselves and with *rear view* to previous conditions to adjust our interpersonal relations using if-then-rules – so to say by *science* (like Aristotle defines it); to cautiously (with *foresight* and *precaution*) or *anxiously* venture on something by *groping* our way, if we do not know, whether we meet something *continuous*-calculable or *discontinuous*-incalculable, demands our *craftsmanship* as a *teleological self*, to bring some succession of activities batched from bottom to top to a good end; if we have *heard* of some attraction and partly *suffering* long for it (hearing is the first sense for great distances), because we are separated from it, in a *prudent* way as an *intentional self* we strive for that, what has been presented to us in *prospect*, and sometimes we reach our goal straight or *linearly*, but sometimes we turn around in a *circle* and must start from scratch again and again; if then, perhaps with *shame*, we *look*, what we have done, and ask ourselves or get questioned by other ones, if we have been *circumspective* enough and have acted with *wisdom*, we often ascertain that we have done something at the wrong *time* or in the wrong *place*, as a *representational self* we maybe have acted according to a system of values, which *represents* our world, and which is *temporally* well adapted, but *spatially* rather inflexible, so that e.g. we hardly get our bearings in other cultures, or we design a corresponding value system everywhere, but then we do not know, when which value is valid now, i.e. our *temporal* orientation has gone.

Regarding Tanabe, I felt touched first of all by his dialectic (Tanabe, 2011) that the modes of being-there, of the individual as a single one, of the species as a special one, and of the genus resp.

---

[3] Mind that learning always has something to do with seeing (sight, view, -spect from Latin spectare, to look)!

part of the communality as a general one, that these modes stand in the relation of an absolute dialectic, i.e. that one of them mediates between the other two, and these together convey the first one. By this, none of the three modes can be preferred. Further on, he points up the mind as the aspect of return to the absolute nothing and the matter as the aspect of alienation from it. I then added a third aspect, the psyche as the dynamic aspect of the absolute nothing, so that we get another absolute conveyance between psyche, mind, and matter, and none of these three aspects can be preferred. By this, the one-sided positions of Freud, Hegel, and Marx regarding these three aspects are destructed. Freud gave priority of his analysis to the psychic-motivational by reducing the origin of everything to the dynamic of our seizedness of our instinctive wishes, Hegel confined himself to the mindful-idealistic, meaning our ideas and expectations, and Marx saw the cause of everything in the alienation resp. in the material aspect that the exploiter deludes the exploited one, concerning certain polarities. But, because of my restatement of Heidegger's concern ("Sorge"), the essence of our being-there is seizedness as well as expectation as well as delusion, and none of them can be preferred because of their absolute dialectical conveyance. Later, Tanabe's absolute dialectic inspired me to realize this relation in the structures of perception, namely space, time, and rhythm, and in the structures of being-there, namely spatiality, timeliness, and reality of life resp. belongingness to the world.

If you group such concepts that way in each case that they relate to each other in an absolute dialectical conveyance, you can see that there are no genuine opposites, so that they are not material (material means perceptible, to perceive is to distinguish, and only there, where there are genuine opposites, you can distinguish), and because of this, you must not objectify resp. hypostatize them.

1.3. Stanley Cavell's Claim of Reason

When I worked through Cavell's magnum opus (Cavell, 1979), which over long distances deals with, how reasonable is the attitude of the skeptic, whereby he assumes that this one must have had some disappointment, I came to the interpretation, the disappointment could be an experience of abuse in one's own family (Kolb, 2012b). By this, the skepticism of the recognitional theorist becomes the claim of or even the cry for love. Insofar that my analysis of being-there deals with the practice of seizedness, of expectation, and especially of delusion, the engagement in Cavell's work was very important for me.

Ending tragically in isolation the skeptic is confronted with the question "Who am I?", which he has the two contradictory answers to, "I am I" and "I am not-I". "That I am I thus says that I am not even me – a hilarious, or rather an ecstatic, glimpse at the possibility that I am not exhausted by all the definitions or descriptions the world gives of me to me." (Cavell, 1979, S. 390) This reminded me of an essay of Ueda (Ueda, 2011): if I stay with the "I am I", then "hate against other ones, basic blindness about oneself and greed" (ibidem, p. 442, own translation) can develop, the "threefold self-poisoning [...] as the basic wrongness and reason of the bane of men" (ibidem, own translation). In the contradictive answer there is "a basic turn around like in »Die and Become Vivid« or in »Death and Resurrection«" (ibidem, p. 443, own translation). By this the ecstasy of future is addressed ("glimpse at the possibility", see above Cavell).

In a corresponding manner the question "What is life?" leads us to the two answers "Life is flowing and blooming by itself, life is living out of its own, life is life" and "Life is not-life" with the ecstasy of origin resp. the character of having been according to Heidegger, namely where all life is coming from, since "nature [...] is the first resurrection body of the unselfish self out of nowhere" (ibidem, own translation).

The question "Who or what is somebody else?" gets the answers "Somebody else is different" and "Somebody else is not different", and this can project us into the ecstasy of arrival resp. present tense according to Heidegger, the presence of the other one, we are confronted with. "The communio of the joint life is the second resurrection body of the self-less self" (ibidem, p. 445, own translation).

This is about "the delivering of the self, from self to self" (ibidem, p. 446, own translation) and by this about the question encompassing the previous ones "What is love?" with the two answers "Understanding is understanding, accepting is accepting, love is love" and "Love is not-love": if I stay with the "Love is love", then a self-consciousness can be established to have loved other ones and possibly by that to have saved them, what would ruin everything, and like above, too, "hate against other ones [, who possibly did not want to be loved by me], basic blindness about oneself and greed" (ibidem, p. 442, own translation) can develop, the "threefold self-poisoning [...] as the basic wrongness and reason of the bane of men" (ibidem, own translation). This experience of loving "proves itself in allowing to awake somebody else, so much so that he himself will awake" (ibidem. P. 445, own translation). He who wants to allow somebody else to awake, will "not preach, not teach, but ask simple questions while meeting as well as while being together: »Where are you from?«, »What′s your name?«, »How are you?«, »Have you had a meal?«, »Do you see these flowers?«" (ibidem, p. 445 f., own translation). So, he asks for quite simple information like Socrates, "and for the other one the question of himself, of his true self is raised: »Who am I intrinsically?«" (ibidem, p. 446, own translation) By this, the ecstasy of information is addressed. For the absolute nothing resp. for perfect love, it is "about the delivering of the self, from self to self" (ibidem, own translation). The delivering from self to self in my opinion is the third resurrection body of the self-less self. By this, the whole processuality is encompassed (see above 1.1) and thus the whole sense of being, i.e. the question of the sense of being is equivalent to the question of love.

The second half of Cavell′s "The Claim of Reason" is more and more about the bodily aspect and its relation to psyche and mind, but here psyche and mind are not clearly distinguished. On the one hand he deals with Wittgenstein′s thesis that the "human body [... would be] the best picture of the human psyche" (Wittgenstein, 2001, S. 1002, PU 496, own translation), on the other hand the body also can be an obstacle to recognize the psyche. For the latter opinion Cavell puts forth a myth (Cavell, 1979, p. 380 et seqq.), which in my opinion symbolically describes the situation of a human being, who was misused in his or her child-hood.

Whether the human body now shows psyche and mind or not, Cavell changes this question into: "Is the cover of skepticism – the conversion of metaphysical finitude into intellectual lack – a denial of the human or an expression of it?" (ibidem, p. 493) It is obviously an expression of the human to deny the human. This, Cavell shows, often becomes a topic e.g. in the tragedies and comedies of Shakespeare:

Since in tragedies death always plays a big role, Cavell again and again returns to "the idea and fate of the human body in these stories" (ibidem, p. 478). In "The Merchant of Venice" by Shakespeare Shylock makes himself a devil's advocate by demanding, Antonio should give him one pound of his flesh in compensation for the psychic defamation, which he had done to Shylock. By this, he wants to demonstrate, how Antonio and the other Christians misuse the analogy between body and psyche, namely if they feel psychically damaged by a Jew, they kill him for that. Shylock, the Jew, and Antonio and his friends, the Christians, deny the human by their cruelty, but at the same time express something very human, namely the need for compensation. Ontologically-intrinsically here, the anger about the thrownness of the being-there is reflected, namely that again and again it is expected to put up with situations, which it is thrown in.

By Shakespeare's "The Winter's Tale" and his "The Tragedy of Othello, the Moor of Venice" Cavell chooses a "second, [...] final illustration [...] of the body's fate under skepticism" (ibidem, p. 481), according to my interpretation when having been abused or blistered. The connection between both pieces "is a tale of harrowing by jealousy, and a consequent accusation for adultery, an accusation known by every outsider, everyone but the accuser, to be insanely false" (ibidem). The harrowing by jealousy is "a harrowing of the power of knowing the existence of another (as chaste, intact, as what the knower knows his other to be). Leontes refuses to believe a true oracle, Othello insists upon believing a false one" (ibidem). Further on, "in both plays the consequence for the man's refusal of knowledge of his other is an imagination of stone" (ibidem, p. 481 f.). Hermione appears as a statue and is accepted as such by Leontes, and Othello describes Desdemona´s skin as "smooth, as a monumental alabaster" (ibidem, p. 482). Apparently, somebody is accepted as human being only then, when he or she has died, but dead and petrified the body is not a human being any more. Ontologically-intrinsically here, on the one hand the fear of death is reflected by the horror, but on the other hand also the suffering from being separated from one´s intrinsic self, thus from perfect love, which is shown by deficiencies to know about the existence of the other one, reflected by the pain. The affect of pain not to be worth to be loved, was stronger for Othello than the fear of death, which he totally had blocked out, so that he killed himself in this affect. The tension (Latin intentio), if he is worth to be loved by Desdemona, was disrupted, and the pain therefore disrupted him. As a tragic hero thus, he may appear to us worth to be loved again. Concretely-ontically the suffering from being separated from my ideal self can become apparent to me by that I think myself not being lovable. Therapeutically sometimes the following affirmation can help here: "I am not perfect, but lovable."

With suffering, it is not only about my *existence*, but also about my *integrity* as human being. Because of my deficiencies, of my imperfectness, for my integrity I am seemingly dependent on that the other one must be seen by me as perfect in his existence, so that his existence is "producing me »in some sense, in [its] own image«" (ibidem, p. 483) providing me with integrity. Typically for a little child this is its mother or father, for Othello it was Desdemona, and by her death the integrity of Othello was destroyed, so that he, after having realized this, also ruined his own existence in his suicide.

2. Philosophical Image of Humanity

Incidentally I want to outline the most important points, which characterize my philosophical image of humanity, which I have presented and elaborated substantially more detailed in my three books "Dasein, um zu lieben" (Kolb, 2017a), "Rhythmus, Intuition und Liebe" (Kolb, 2017b), and "Liebe, Macht und Sexualität" (Kolb, 2017c).

2.1. Basics of My Analysis of Being-There

As already explained in "Dasein, um zu lieben" (Kolb, 2017a), our being-there as humans has on the one hand the mode of communal being, which I want to call genus following Tanabe (Tanabe, 2011), on the other hand the mode of individual being, I call individuum, and finally the mode of special being or species (ibidem), if we are in certain positions and exercise special functions, namely act in special relations with others and as a part of special structures in our community. As communal being we conceive, what we have perceived resp. distinguished (<u>differentiation</u>) – for that we principally need other people, in the beginning of our being-there our mother as the main caregiver –, where it comes from, i.e. we are projected and shall later project ourselves into the ecstasy of origin (the character of having been, "Gewesenheit", according to Heidegger (Heidegger, 2006a)), to conceive the conditions of the situation and to <u>integrate</u> them into an overall impression; as individual being we theoretically understand ourselves as skilled at, what we have conceived and what we are seized with by that – in this we principally are isolated, must consider and plan for ourselves, at most can borrow suggestions from other ones, initially from our mother –, i.e. because of corresponding expectations we are projected resp. shall later project ourselves into the ecstasy of future, to decide upon an action, which is believed to operate in a <u>regulating</u> manner; as species we expectantly perform, what we have considered, planned, and decided, we understand ourselves as practically skilled – in this we principally are estranged from ourselves, must act on ourselves, at most can borrow some practical advices and exemplary behavior from others, initially from our mother –, i.e. because of corresponding actions and results we are projected resp. shall later project ourselves into the ecstasy of arrival (or present tense according to Heidegger), to deal with the consequences of our actions. By the ecstasy of information, what comes out, if we have got a certain managing with the world, – this is the important link Heidegger has overlooked – we again come into the mode of genus, and the spiral of development goes on.

Moreover, there are the aspects of being-there, the bodily-material one marked by affects, dichotomies, accordances and delusions, the psychic-motivational one marked by sensations and the dynamic of seizedness, and the mindful-idealistic one marked by feelings and presentations/imaginations of ideals and catastrophes resp. expectations. In the mode of genus we are objects of the bodily-material aspect, perceiving and distinguishing, and psychic motivated subjects, who, together with other ones conceive and mean to know the score, in the mode of individuum sensing objects of our seizedness, i.e. of the psychic-motivational aspect, and mindful subjects, who consider, plan and decide, and in the mode of species we are objects of our expectations, feeling forward, thus of the mindful-idealistic aspect, and bodily-material subjects, who actively deal with the dichotomies of matter. Altogether here, there is a circle, which can be passed through in two directions. I shall revert to this topic further below, when I am concerned with the different memory processes.

When we, together with Heidegger, ask for the sense of being, then in the end it is about a meaningful fabric, a structure, and the timeliness found by him is such a structure. On the one hand you can distinguish structures of being-there, namely timeliness, spatiality, and reality of life resp. belongingness to the world, on the other hand the corresponding structures of perceiving, as there are time, space, and rhythm. These both groups of three structures each I have chosen, because they convey each other absolutely dialectically according to the definition of Tanabe. To perceive means to distinguish, so the structures of perception allow us to distinguish things that matter, while by the structures of being-there we are required to use the differences, which are opened to us resp. which we can open. Thus by the one-dimensional time, we are required to project ourselves into the three temporal ecstasies origin, future, and arrival, by the three-dimensional space to go into the one ecstasy of information by letting ourselves in for the exchange with other people and inter-action with other things, whom or which we meet in the world, and by rhythm with its dynamic, its interfering contact, and its ef-fective turn, which altogether results in a similarly recurrent rhythmical gestalt, by the swelling-up-and-down pulsating we are required to let ourselves in for the reality of life resp. for our re-lation with our being in the world, as I call our life, resp. to let ourselves in for being in the world and for simply belonging to it. In so far, the structures of time and timeliness correspond to the aspect of the mindful-idealistic, because ideals and goals need time, until they are realized or reached, space and spatiality are related to the bodily-material, because opposites need a place to unfold, and rhythm and reality of life resp. belonging to the world refer to the dynamic of the psychic-motivational, which moves us and makes us vivid. If we take our time giving space to the world, we enable vividness.

As individuum the being-there is quite in the in-oneself, quite on one's own, because the burden of one's sensational states of mind as object of the psyche nobody can take over ("We all have our crosses to bear"), and nobody can challenge one for one's dignity as a drafting one, as a mindful subject ("Thoughts are free"). As an individual being the being-there determines one-self completely and utterly, it is completely and utterly singular, drafting full of expectations and of sensitively seized thrownness (free according to Heidegger, 2006a). With one's burden and dig-nity one's holistic self-understanding is opened to the being-there as individuum, even if not necessarily intelligible. A *perfect holistic self-understanding* is, what in an ideal way signalizes the mode of individuum.

As species the being-there is quite in the off-oneself, com-ing out of one's in-oneself and approaching one's environment, contacting it, because with one's intention to execute a certain possibility of one's capability-to-be one approaches one's environment with something of oneself as something special, one brings something special to the attention of one's environment in a special way, and by the actual executing as a material subject, there will develop interaction and contact. While the plan of one's capability-to-be still was a part of oneself, that, what arises during the contact with one's environment, is strange to one, the action generates the movement of self-alienation, if you label the other one or the environment as strange. As species the being-there determines one's environment completely and utterly and in the ideal case acts effectively and only because of one's own expectations, but often also because of expectations of others. *Autonomy and effectivity* are, what in an ideal way signalizes the mode of species.

As genus the being-there is in a movement from the strange back to oneself by perceiving the strange, the result of the contact, by one's senses as object of matter and thereby re-acting positively, if the expectations are fulfilled, negatively, if not, and with more or less neutral or ambivalent affect, if partly fulfilled and partly not, to selectively look at the perceived as a psychic subject in some circumstances together with others, to conceive (to thus understand the perceived in its conditionality), and so to make it a part of oneself again as the affectively con-ceived understanding in form of a representation of reality and of an outlook towards the world and other ones. I call this conceiv-ing therefore affectively conceiving understanding, because the being-there as object of matter always gets pleasant or unpleas-ant affects together with one's perception, and by this one al-ready can discover immediate consequences of one's behavior, and thus a first conceiving is enabled. By this, the being-there as genus is both in the in-oneself and in the off-oneself, thus in the in-and-off-oneself. One is completely and utterly in an interactive and communicative exchange with the world and other ones, in an affectively conceiving understanding, and thus is completely and utterly a general being, one is in an expressing-impressing making-one's-own of reality in form of certain representations. After a corresponding deed, the being-there can conceive as a ge-nus, if and how far one has succeeded in overcoming delusions resp. the dichotomies of matter both for oneself and in the ideal case equally for others in a solidary way. The *communicative solidarity* (Rentsch, 1999, S. 258) is, what in an ideal way signalizes the mode of genus. In what way here, I can speak of an ideal in each case, this shall make clear the following consideration:

2.2. The Utopia of Perfect Love

If we want to analyze something, then we purpose something, we want to improve something in any respect. An analysis of being-there cannot be executed without an aim, as well as "a philosophical (not an empirical) anthropology cannot be conceptualized pre- or extra-ethically" (Rentsch, 1999, p. 1, own translation). To improve our human being-there, the perfect overcoming of all delusions resp. dichotomies of matter offers itself as goal resp. as ideal, because then and only then our seizedness/conceiving and our expectations are congruent, and we find our being-there fulfilled. Psyche and mind are in absolute harmony, i.e. as individuum we understand our corresponding seizedness, the for-the-sake-of-which, truly and immediately. "Truly" means that there is no delusion, and "immediately" that the sensational state of mind of seizedness resp. the for-the-sake-of-which is understood just like that, without any conveyance of anything else but the seizedness itself, thus without any concepts, outlooks, or other representations of reality. Then and only then the delusions are perfectly overcome, i.e. only the true and immediate understanding of the seizedness is equivalent with the perfect overcoming of delusions, because an understanding, which is conveyed by anything and thus a conveyed overcoming of delusions, is dependent on the conveyance and hence possibly instable, in each case however not perfect.

When seizedness/conceiving and expectation are congruent resp. without delusion, then the affect of being-there as object of matter is pure pleasure, and as psychic subject it is so much satisfied that one creates no more representations of reality, since one also is in perfect harmony with all others. Thus, holistic self-understanding and communicative solidarity are in an absolute consonance, because our seizedness comes from that, what we have conceived as genus and psychic subject in the communicative solidarity with others.

True means that the understanding arrives at no plan and thus the being-there to no action, which leads to a delusion. Since no deed or action as species is needed to overcome a delusion or disappointment (this is a sensation because of conceiving the perception of a delusion as not fulfilled expectation), each deed is neither technically useful nor hypothetically pleasant, but categorical in terms of Kant or unintentional in terms of Taoism (wu wei, doing in calmness, without having to regulate something, doing in not-doing), and therefore also absolutely autonomic and effective, and the being-there understands oneself altogether, i.e. autonomy and effectiveness and holistic self-understanding are in absolute consonance.

Since there are no delusional dichotomies of matter, as genus, there are no self-alienation and no more conflicts with other ones, i.e. perfect harmony prevails with oneself and with all other human beings. This is exactly then the case, when in all of one's relations with other ones, there is an absolute egality between us, and an absolute freedom in each relation. Absolute egality is to mean here that I understand the other one and myself equally in each for-the-sake-of-which in a true and immediate manner, else there would be no perfect harmony, and absolute freedom says here that for my sake everybody can absolutely freely resp. autonomously and thus effectively act, else my harmony would be instable and not perfect. Autonomy and effectivity and communicative solidarity are in absolute consonance. Thus, when reaching this utopian goal of the perfect overcoming of all delusion and dichotomies, I would truly and immediately understand the for-the-sake-of-which of my own individual being-there and that of the being-there of all others I would meet. This goal I want to call *perfect love*. It includes perfect self-love and perfect love of others likewise.

Utopian goals are reasonable only then, when steady progress and corresponding improvements are possible, and when it is inherent in the being-there, even if the goal remains unattainable. Then the way is the goal. How the way to perfect love may look, and that the utopian goal of perfect love is inherent in us, I have revealed in "Dasein, um zu lieben" (Kolb, 2017a). Since only in matter the delusions and dichotomies are perceptible, there you can see the distance to resp. the alienation of perfect love as the material moment or aspect of it. If formally you assume that perfectness has been prevailing, once still there did not exist any being-there, and if you accept perfect love as ideal, then mind is the aspect of return to perfect love, its mindful moment. Then the psyche you can call the dynamic resp. the psychic-motivational aspect or moment of perfect love. Thus, psyche, mind, and matter are the three aspects of perfect love, and therefore, the being-there with its basic aspects psyche, mind, and body is a picture of perfect love.

By this, perfect love is *"universal-anthropological"* (Rentsch, 1999, p. 306, own translation). When here with me, the way is made the goal and perfect love is labeled as a utopian goal, then this is due to the imperfectness and fragility of being-there, what calls for realistic inter-goals, and here the ethos as momentary mentuality or prereflexive knowledge has its place. Also, Aristotle's "eudaimonia" as ultimate sense of the entire human life corresponds to the goal of perfect love. All typical human of any actions, which extend the animalistic, strives for understanding and for long-ranging, especially verbal exchange with other humans, and thus for perfect love, which by that only is established as a human performance-gestalt or "telos". The typical human is neither instrumental resp. technically useful nor hedonistic resp. hypothetically pleasant, but according to Aristotle has its sense by itself resp. is categorical in terms of Kant and by this reasonable. Since perfect love is a utopian goal, which the being-there again and again strives for, as long as one lives, its determination "cannot be made below the niveau of a *Lebensform* (a gestalt, which encompasses the human life as a whole)" (ibidem, p. 298, own translation). The way to perfect love can be gone only in the interaction and communication with others and "belongs as such to the context of the communicative communal life, and it is not that it can be determined »subjectively«" (ibidem, own translation).

If you take perfect love for true and immediate understanding of the for-the-sake-of-which of each being-there, then (1) in the immediacy, the timeliness is overcome and the <u>pure</u> (simply immediate) <u>mindful drafting</u> without regarding origin, future and arrival is achieved, (2) in the trueness, which provides no place for doubts, the spatiality as challenge to embark is overcome and the <u>pure</u> (simply true) <u>bodily encounter</u> without doubting reluctance toward others or the world is reached, and finally (3) without any seizedness resp. without any for-the-sake-of-which, what the work shall serve for and what it shall reach, the reality of life is overcome and the <u>pure</u> (simply lively working resp. excitingly seizing), the being-in-the-world approving <u>motivation</u> is gained by the now fulfilled <u>psyche</u>.

As in "Dasein, um zu lieben" pointed out, this way of being-there means the absolute self-negation all in one with the absolute self-affirmation. Further, the way to perfect love is the absolute negation (of all the aspects) of being-there. At the end of this way, both the three modes individuum, species, genus and the three aspects psyche, mind, matter have crumbled away, and the being-there has come to nothing. At least, it is no more from this world resp. has nothing to do with any concept of anything. On the other hand, the being-there then affirms one´s existence absolutely. Dedication and admission, giving and taking, affirmation and negation become one. Still, to exaggerate the confusion: in perfect love all the three aspects and thus the existence of being-there are absolutely unimportant and meaningless. Since this is valid for the three aspects of perfect love, this means, we should not concentrate on the perfectness of our love, this is meaningless for us. To develop our ability to love more and more, this way is the goal.

As a mathematician I would say, the way to perfect love is a non-convergent sequence with no determinable limit value in infinity. The state of perfect love is absolutely indeterminable for us. The way to this leads into the infinite, and this is no more from this world, so that here, it becomes intelligible that this way is the absolute negation of our world and leads to something, which is in principle not determinable. By going this way however, we affirm this world, without which we could not go this way. On the other hand, by concentrating on this way, the world gets more and more meaningless. In some absolutely indeterminable manner psyche, mind, and matter are absolutely united because of an absolute dedication, admission and meaninglessness, some sort of triunity. For "absolutely" we also could take the expression "infinitely". Thus, you could interpret the human being-there as a projection of this infinite intangible into the finite, as a picture of this, and in principle there are infinitely many pictures of this.

From this conception it results that the two following courses of action strengthen our ability to love: (1) pardoning (not to take something personal[4] for evil, so that the past of being-there sinks into meaninglessness, since only something personal is meaningful), (2) giving and holding promises, thus dedicating the future of being-there. These two, according to Hannah Arendt, help solving the two basic problems of interhuman action better and better, namely the imponderability and the irrevocability (Arendt, 1998), so that we more and more gratefully can accept our everyday life, the present moment of being-there. Because of this meaninglessness of the past, of this dedication of the future, and of this grateful acceptance of the present, pardoning and promising resp. declaring commitments are acts of love, and the better we succeed in solving problems of interhuman action, the more perfect is our love. As acts of love they foster both the communicative solidarity and the effectivity of any autonomous acting, and in order not to take something personally for evil, we need a corresponding self-understanding. The heavier or deeper we are affected or hurt and aggrieved in our behavior, the deeper and more perfect our self-understanding must be, in order that we do no more take it personally evil to the other person. Deeds you cannot pardon, only the perpetrator in this sense. Thus, my

---

[4] Here personality means the image, others make themselves of us from the total impression, they have got about us. Our self is the total impression, we have got about ourselves, our Ego (or I) is, what just comes forward as our own impression of ourselves for the moment, occasionally also vociferously, and our person or our authentic self is, what we suppose behind all our expressions, what "sounds through" through all our appearances (from Latin per-sonare). "Personal" means this authentic.

definition of love might be made sufficiently intelligible and understandable.

In order that the being-there reaches the way to perfect love and comes forward on it, in "Dasein, um zu lieben" I found three necessary and together sufficient conditions: again and again, to strive for true information about the origin of the momentary situation, for true information about the future of the possibilities of the capability-to-be in the momentary situation, and for true information about the arrival in the momentary situation[5]. By this, you will gradually come to develop a stronger and stronger communicative solidarity, a bigger and bigger holistic self-understanding and a more and more encompassing autonomy and effectivity, and by this the being-there succeeds better and better to regulate one's emotions (affects, sensations, and feelings), what in turn makes one's striving for true information more successful, so that one progresses more and more on the way to perfect love. During this, one recognizes more and more the meaninglessness of one's earlier existence, becomes more and more ready to dedicate one's future existence, e.g. by giving and holding promises, and all in one accepts by this one's momentary existence more and more gratefully.

Whatever demands us concretely resp. ontically in our relation to our momentary being-in-the-world to solve problems, in a deeper sense resp. ontologically it is always about, how we develop our capability to love and thus make more and more progress on the way to perfect love. Thereby, the problem may be on the one hand that the intrinsic sensation of anxiety in terms of Heidegger bothers us, if we cannot or do not want to bear this and the principle disclosedness of the unsurpassability of our death resp. of our mortality together with the corresponding

---

[5] A situation is a spatiotemporal conceived context regarding some goal resp. some for-the-sake-of-which, in which a living being, within certain spatial and temporal boundaries resp. horizons, can distinguish resp. perceive material opposites, judge prospects (what may come towards it) and conclude practical connections, both inductively and deductively, as well as conductively, where something generally comes from, where something specially leads to, and where you in a single case get brought together resp. conducted with.

helplessness, on the other hand, the intrinsic sensation of anger may hold us back or even block us on this way, if this anger and the principle disclosedness of the irreducibility of our thrownness resp., which conditions of being-there have been forced on us, overexert and overrun us with all its might. Thirdly, our way to perfect love can be aggrieved or obstructed by that the intrinsic sensation of suffering and the principle disclosedness of our being-separated from our authentic self, thus from perfect love, the not-at-home ("Unzuhause") like Heidegger calls this being-separated, and that the related hopelessness is totally energy-sapping.

On the other side, the intrinsic sensation of joy, the pleasure, how Aristotle calls it, which is not confronted by an unpleasure or aversion to be compensated – otherwise this sensation would not be intrinsic resp. no sensation, but a feeling connected with some concrete expectation – this pleasure can give us the necessary power despite being separated from our authentic self, meaning from perfect love, the necessary courage in spite of the big challenge, and the necessary trust and patience in spite of our mortality, so that we make steady progress on the way to perfect love.

In "Sein und Zeit" Heidegger has, as he writes, picked out the "basic sensational state of mind of anxiety as a distinguished disclosedness of being-there" (Heidegger, 2006a, p. 184, own translation), whereby he never claimed that anxiety would be the only basic sensational state of mind of this kind. But by this, it came to an imbalance of his analysis of being-there, because he concentrated only on anxiety, death, and future. For the phenomenal raising of the analysis I have included in the analysis of being-there the other, in my opinion equally important and basic sensational states of mind of anger, because of our thrownness into irreducible conditions, of suffering, because of our being-separated from our authentic self, from perfect love, and of joy, when we move further towards the goal of perfect love. These four basic sensational states of mind are equiprimordial and constitute the primordial phenomenon of sensational states of mind. "The phenomenon of *equiprimordiality* of the constituting moments often has been neglected according to a methodically rampant tendency to verify the origin of all and everybody from some simple »primal ground«." (Heidegger, 2006a, p. 131, own translation) By over-emphasizing the anxiety, Heidegger contradicted himself.

2.3. The Memory and Its Functions

One important point of view I did not consider for my analysis up to now, which deals with the temporal ecstasy of origin resp. the character of having been according to Heidegger, namely our reflexivity, which on the one hand helps to handle earlier incidents later, which maybe we have not yet conceived, so that this, our earlier existence more and more can sink into meaninglessness. On the other hand, this reflexivity more and more can take horror of gruesome things from us, which still may come towards us, by comparing them with earlier experiences. Symbolically the Greek expressed this by the myth of Perseus, who could look at the heads of the three medusas undamaged only by a reflecting mirror without turning into stone. Further, because of our reflexivity we can be conscious in the here and now. In "Liebe, Macht und Sexualität" (Kolb, 2017c), in the 9th chapter I denoted consciousness as a state of the capability to compare, and to be conscious, to be able to compare, we only can because of our reflexivity. Concretely or ontically, our reflexivity shows up in the content of our memory.

As an object of matter, psyche, and mind the being-there, since one is reflexive and is about one's being, needs some sort of memory respectively, which I called memory of affects, memory of sensations, and memory of feelings in "Liebe, Macht und Sexualität". If we perceive something, this relates to an affect, it affects us, turns us on, so that we notice it and memorize it in the memory of affects. If then we conceive this and realize, what it matters to us, we sense, find ourselves, since we are concerned, and memorize it in the memory of sensations. If then we sensationally understand, which possibilities of our capability to be we can draft, then feelings relate to the corresponding expectations, we feel forward, which affects and sensations we would have, if the expected arrives resp. gets fulfilled. This we memorize in the memory of feelings. Affects, sensations, and feelings are in an absolutely dialectical conveyance according to Tanabe, so that you may call them emotions altogether and summarize the three kinds of memory as emotional memory.

Correspondingly we also are reflexive, each as bodily-material, psychic-motivational, and mindful-idealistic subjects with three kinds of memory, namely the action and effect memory, the condition and concept memory, and the planning memory as described in "Liebe, Macht und Sexualität". These three kinds of memory correspond to the three modes species, genus, and individuum of being-there and are in an absolutely dialectical conveyance, too, so that you may summarize them as autobiographic memory – autobiographic, because thus we ourselves (auto = self) reflexively record (graphein = to record) our previous relation to our being-in-the-world, that is our life (bios = life), in our memory. Since however, we notice life dates of others which we empathetically identify ourselves with, too, this is rather a biographic memory.

Now, the interesting thing is, how these different kinds of memory interact with each other, because by this analysis you can very well work out the different mechanisms of suppression, namely separation, defense, and coping (see below), which, seen ontologically, let us know in some different manner, how we may hinder ourselves or may be blocked on our way to perfect love. Up to now, I only have looked at disturbances on the way to perfect love from the side of being-there as subject, when because of anxiety, anger, or suffering, each as intrinsic sensations, we correspondingly do not decisively strive for true information about future (anxiety), origin (anger) and arrival (suffering) any more, and do not connect the contents of the biographic memory with the emotional one. Now, it is about the consideration of being-there as object of psyche, mind, and matter, if we do not process contents of the emotional memory and integrate them in the biographic one.

If we look at the development of children, first on the level of the physical self (Fonagy, Gergely, Jurist, & Target, 2004) by *insight* (Kolb, 2017c) they learn to connect certain affective perceptions with activities, i.e. a connection is established from the affect memory to the action memory, which is only a memory of some activities and their effects at this point of time. On the level of the social self, by *rear view* resp. regard (ibidem) the children learn to include certain conditions sensationally, so that they create connections from the sensation memory to the condition and concept memory, and from this to the affect memory (ibidem). On the level of the teleological self by *foresight* resp. precaution (ibidem) children learn to understand certain possibilities sensationally, so that they create connections from the action memory to the feeling memory and from there to the planning memory, which at first was a memory of possibilities and only on the next level, the one of the intentional self, becomes the planning memory (ibidem). Now, the circle gets closed by learning by *prospect* (ibidem), while a connection from the planning memory to the sensational memory develops, so that children can gain more and more prudent views, which conditions must be fulfilled and which risks and chances there are. Therefore, I called this circle the *circle of prudent action* (ibidem). Here you can realize that and how biographic contents of memory get combined with emotional ones. Up to this, many mammals and some other animals like birds can develop.

Only with the reverse, the reflection of this circle because of learning by *circumspect* (ibidem) on the level of the representational self the typical human arises, namely the circle of circumspective or responsible acting, only then that comes out, what Aristotle calls the virtue of wisdom. Only here we human beings ask ourselves questions like: Do I have enough regards? Is the prospect worthwhile? Am I cautious enough? Do I have enough capabilities and attainments? Do I have enough insight? Should I circumspect more? When is enough enough? If you call philosophy the realm of human being-there, in which you ask yourself basic questions and look for basic answers, then you can say that we human beings become philosophers since this stage of development, indeed must be philosophers (lovers of wisdom, lovers of love, since love is the ultimate wisdom), else we would not be human.

Because of each of our activities as subject, the contents of the emotional memory are handled further on and integrated in the autobiographic memory, by connecting them with the corresponding activity, which we are asked for as object because of the regarding emotion. As long as some content of the emotional memory still is not integrated in the autobiographic memory, we only can remember it by reminding of the previous activity resp. by performing it, an affect by previous specific activities, a sensation by previous conceiving, and a feeling by previous planning. Only then can we progress on the circle of responsible-reflected action. Examples for this you find in the 3rd chapter of "Liebe, Macht und Sexualität" (ibidem).

If we proceed on this circle of human action steadily and decisively, we progress on the way to perfect love, too, so that the question arises, when and by what it comes to the point that there occur difficulties, stalemate, or regresses on this way. If our power of imagination for reality is not strong enough, the affect too fierce, the perceived opposites too big to be able to tackle the situation by conceiving as *genus*, then we are blocked at this point and it comes that we *separate* the affect, the typical mechanism of suppression when traumata occur, or we have compulsions or some sort of psychosis – then we are no more truly in contact with reality, the corresponding affects will not be integrated in the autobiographic memory.

If we do not muster up enough power of imagination for catastrophes and ideals, if our sensations are too strong because of too big conceived dichotomies of matter, so that we cannot deliberate (may I liberate myself?) appropriate possibilities as *individuum* and plan corresponding activities to deal with these dichotomies, because, if we would so, strong feelings of shame would arise because of supposed or known deficiencies, then we defend ourselves against these sensations by pretending to ourselves and others, to be on top of things, and may be develop an inappropriate pride. We then do not have the courage to face up to the different possibilities, which are available, and to the corresponding expectations. So, we *defend* our sensations, the typical mechanism of suppression for addictive disorders. The corresponding sensations will not be integrated in the autobiographic memory.

When in the mode of being-there of *species*, we do not have enough self-confidence, if the negative feeling is too strong because of too big dichotomies, which we imagine together with our corresponding plans, too big to deal practically with them, so that we get strong feelings of failure beforehand, then we try to *cope* with these feelings by distracting ourselves with other specific activities, which seemingly absolutely must be done in advance, or by sinking into apathy, namely capitulate and impassively do not feel anything (it comes to typical utterances like "I cannot manage that" or the like). In psychoanalysis you call this *coping* with feelings, though I find the expression overwhelming more fitting. This is the typical mechanism of suppression for anxieties and depressions. The concrete fear becomes changed back into a diffuse and thus neurotic anxiety, e.g. into a general anxiety of failure. The corresponding feelings will not be integrated in the autobiographic memory.

Big dichotomies on the bodily-material level trigger affects, which occupy space very much and thus lead to a big overstimulation or flooding, so that we separate these affects possibly. If we succeed in not separating, but in conceiving them, then the corresponding sensations cause such a pulsating pressure that we defend them in some cases and do not want them to press us. If despite all, we manage it to sensationally understand that we have possibilities, and correspondingly consider and plan, then we feel such a great time pressure and pressure to achieve that we cope with these feelings by actionism or by apathy as the case may be, and that we cope with this pressure that way (like this, the psychoanalytic expression of coping is fitting), however without adequately dealing with the dichotomies as such. As you see here, all three structures of perception play a role, the space if you separate, the rhythmicity of the living if you defend, and the time if you cope with time pressure resp. pressure to achieve, the pressure of expectations. Correspondingly we do not meet the respective requests of the analogous structures of being-there: when separating we do not exchange with others and do not get involved with our environment by circumspectively act-ing[6], when defending we do not get mixed up with the reality of life, and when coping we do not let ourselves in for projecting ourselves or being projected into the three temporal ecstasies of origin, future, and arrival because of our planning resp. by our ex-pectations.

2.4. Various Types of Getting Knowledge

That getting knowledge generally and therefore espe-cially in psychotherapy is important, I need not emphasize. We principally get knowledge about something by comparing only and thus by consciousness, a state of being able to compare and the process of comparing (Kolb, 2017c, p. 194, chapter 8). The process of getting knowledge performs itself by three ways, de-pending on, what mode our being-there just is in. In the mode of genus as objects of matter we meet its opposites, which we affec-tively realize more and more, and which we can distinguish resp. perceive by that better and better, the further our senses and learnt perceptual patterns are developed. Besides, as psychic sub-jects we are sensitive, at the beginning of our life especially con-cerning sensations of pleasure and unpleasure. Between both (being object or subject) other people convey, at first usually our mother, who deals with the opposites of matter in such ways that we feel as good as possible. These other people lend us their sup-port with words and deeds, in the ideal case with communicative solidarity, as I called it here in section 2.2, and according to our own development we help others correspondingly. In the 11th chapter of "Rhythmus, Intuition und Liebe" (Kolb, 2017b) I called this ensouling and inspiring. Knowledge means here to acquaint oneself with something strange and thus to overcome resp. to deal with the opposite strange-familiar.

---

[6] Traumatized people have disturbances to find words, when they shall report their traumatic experiences.

In the mode of individuum as objects of psyche we meet the dynamic of our sensations, we can deal with better and better, the better we conceive our relation to our environment, also by certain learnt concepts. Besides, as mindful subjects we are capable to draft possibilities of our capability how to be, to consider, and to plan. Between both we ourselves convey, in the ideal case with holistic self-understanding, as I called it here in section 2.2, and according to our own development of our self-understanding. Here knowledge means that we adopt something of the dynamic of our sensations, something of ourselves, make it our own and consider, how to deal best with it, how we judge something in relation to ourselves, if it is our own responsibility or the one of somebody else, which plans we make and what we decide upon.

In the mode of species finally, as objects of mind we are feelingly busy with our imaginations, plans, decisions, and expectations, which we can deal with all the better, the better we understand, how in praxis to implement our purposes, projects, or experiments, the more skilled and the more dexterously we can act as bodily-material subjects, also by learnt action patterns. Here our experiences convey our purposes to their implementation. In the ideal case then, we are autonomous resp. self-determined and effective, as I called it here in section 2.2. Knowledge means here that we more and more let ourselves in for the difficulties of matter, that is for something strange, and handle it practically.

All three types of getting knowledge relate to each other in a natural way, they are together in an absolute dialectical relationship of conveyance. Only if, in the mode of species, I let myself in for something strange, I can make it familiar to me in the mode of genus, by what parts of me get opened, which I can adopt as something of my own in the mode of individuum, by what new possibilities of capabilities how to be break open, so that in the mode of species I can let myself in for something strange in a new way etc. Thus, no type of getting knowledge can be preferred.

For all three types I need trust, confidence, and courage, trust in the human community, confidence in myself, and hope and courage to let myself in for the world that is strange for me.

But there are boundaries, and here we must reflect the circle of development in the previous section to realize these boundaries (her the process of knowledge is reflected, and this leads to knowledge on another level). In the mode of individuum, I should not confide too much in myself and believe, I could care alone for myself and would need nobody else, would not need trust in other people, too. In the mode of genus, I should not only trust in others that they will rescue me and care for me, as if I would not have to let myself in for my life and for the world by active caring, too. And in the mode of species, I should not only hope, I could manage everything without any risk, without attending my knowledge resp. the understanding of myself regarding the boundaries of my skills and dexterities. Where there are the boundaries of confidence in the mode of individuum, this will be compensated by the trust in other people in the mode of genus, the boundaries of which will be balanced by self-determined action, the boundaries of which will be put into the right place by my individual self-assessment etc.

In contrast to Descartes, who tried to handle the opposite inside-outside better and better, and who by this committed himself to a certain image resp. conception of the world, which often has been criticized, in my approach, knowledge deals with the opposites strange-familiar, strange-own, and being passively confronted with something strange or even abandon it vs. self-determined and decisive letting oneself in. In the conception of Descartes, the opposite inside-outside turns to be an insurmountable problem, namely to the problem of transcendence. Thus, phenomena of transcendence, which become obvious, when processes organize themselves, cannot be explained. If e.g. an audience goes into a concerted rhythm of clapping, where is its origin, inside or outside, and if inside or outside, where exactly? This is because with Descartes you only can gain knowledge in the mode of species, if you meet the strange of your environment manifestly, other types of getting knowledge are treated as extensions only, like the exchange with other ones in the mode of genus, or involve the danger of subjective contamination of knowledge, if you cannot completely push aside your own, individual needs and wants, what however is not possible in principle. Thus, we cannot find "a way of understanding ourselves that is not radically self-undermining, and that does not require us to deny the obvious" (Nagel, 2012, p. 25).

On the one hand, it is the merit of Descartes that he shows up: "though one cannot know truth as something given and disclosed, man can at least know what he makes himself" (Arendt, 1998, p. 282), so that people have been encouraged to experiment in the mode of species. This led to enormous scientific progress and knowledge and to many technical performances. On the other hand, it has removed us from the original natural-paradisiac conditions further and further afar, not only regarding our environment at that, which we destroy on and on, but also with respect to the relation of people among themselves: the mistrust of one´s own capability to know turned on the other ones more or less, and thus on common-sense, which turned to be merely the public spirit of a certain community, so that the opinion of the majority was generally dismissed as irrelevant. The hunch of living in a "looking-glass world" is "»the outcome of common-sense in retreat«" (ibidem, p. 283).

The intellectual approach of Descartes engulfs us in a considerably worse dilemma: to know and to realize, what we have done, on one side, opens us many possibilities to shape our life, on the other side, this burdens us with the responsibility for all we have done. In a way, we stand in a quagmire by this: on the one hand, we are summoned to gather more and more knowledge by experiments without, on the other hand, being previously able to know and thus to be responsible for, what we in some circumstances shall bring about by this. This is a similar double bind, as if a mother says to her child: "Develop, learn, try out, and do only, what I deem right!" On one side, it is required from a scientist to research autonomously and effectively and not to engage in anything, on the other side, he shall do nothing, what people deem dangerous, i.e. here after all, he shall engage and abide by rules of somebody else.

By my conception, the opposites strange-familiar, strange-own, and being passively confronted with something strange or abandon it vs. self-determined and decisive letting oneself in, are considerably more flexible than the opposite in-side-outside, and insofar they adapt themselves much better to vivid processes, where something strange can get familiar, but also something familiar strange, where you can prove your own responsibility, and identify with something strange, and deidenti-fy from something you have deemed your own, and where you can let yourself in on something strange you meet, but also again abandon it. Knowledge is not exclusively conveyed in one single mode, since all three mentioned types of getting knowledge are equitably placed side by side. By this the double bind mentioned above is widely defused.

The contents of our knowledge are manifold interwoven, and you cannot differentiate them in elements clearly isolated from each other as you can do by the cartesian conception of the world. The phenomenon of self-organizing processes proves that the total is more than the sum of its single parts, and not com-pletely reducible to it. The reduction to so called atoms, meaning undividable elements, cannot be successful, this also shows the science of atom physics, which has come from atoms to the so-called elementary particles (electrons, protons, and neutrons), to quarks and finally to strings, and there is no prospect of an end.

The interweaving of contents of knowledge corresponds distinctly better to the world, how it befalls us as vivid nature, the parts of which you can classify neither into pure ideas ("res cogi-tantes") nor into pure material things, to the cartesian "res exten-sae". The sensation of pain is reducible neither to an idea nor to a mechanical or physico-chemical cause. This each doctor knows, who had a medical result of a patient, where this man should have great pain – that was the doctor's idea – but the patient had no pain, or conversely, there was no result, but the patient suffered pain. Also, there are no immediate circumstances, nothing in the world is absolute, everything is somehow related to each other and thus relative. The world and we ourselves as parts of the world are anything else but machines.

Corresponding to the classification of our getting knowledge, our thinking can be regarded as a dialectical one in the mode of genus, an abstract one in the mode of individuum, and an analytic one in the mode of species (Kolb, 2017e, p. 57 et seqq., 4th chapter). First, the dialectical thinking serves to realize, who is somebody else, and what is the essential of a situation, next, when abstractly thinking, I judge my own situation and realize by this mostly only indirectly, who am I, and finally, when analytically thinking I conclude according to logical principles, how I can deal with other ones, our situation and with myself as best as possible, and thus realize my actual skills and dexterities.

For the dialectical thinking I need empathy with other ones, to know, who is the other one and how is his situation, when abstractly thinking the same for me, to protect me against false judging, while when analytically thinking, I am distanced, differentiate in single elements, categorize and do not empathy just yet, but look at everything and everybody from a position of a third person, in order that my logical conclusions will not be tarnished by the interests of others or by my own ones. The latter is the scientific outlook, which has developed from the cartesian conception of the world, and which a corresponding mechanistic image of the world underlies.

If you look more exactly, how some knowledge is achieved in the three modes of being-there, various rhythms and resonances play the decisive role when perceiving with our senses. When hearing and seeing, this is perfectly obvious, and when touching or sensing temperature, biophysics tells us the facts. That this is even the case when smelling and tasting, the results from quantum biology show (Al-Khalili & McFadden, 2014). For all living beings both phenomena, rhythm and resonance, play a central role as far down as the cellular level: Al-Khalili and McFadden argue that living cells and thus all living beings could not exist without using quantum effects like tunneling and non-locality (ibidem). In order that you can use quantum effects, meaning that you preserve the necessary coherence long enough, the wave character of the subatomic structures (electrons, protons, and the like) must be protected. When solving this problem technically, e.g. when constructing quantum computers, one shields corresponding gadgets as much as possible and reduces temperature nearby to the absolute zero point. Living beings seem to have found another solution: on the one hand, they keep the "thermodynamic rustling" (chaotic vibrations because of temperature) in the frame of a so called "white rustling" and as constant as possible – especially animals with a constant temperature of their body –, and they modulate other vibrations, which contrast with this, so that via resonance they support the wave character of the subatomic structures. Therefore, resonance and rhythm play a big role for living beings: whether something is living, e.g. we recognize by, whether some part of it is moving in a rhythmical way. This we can perceive, when we come into resonance with such movements, which we may call impulses then.

By this the contact with other ones, with ourselves and with our environment comes about directly and immediately with rhythm and resonance in all three modes of being-there, so that you may call my epistemology, deduced from my analysis of being-there, a contact theory. Dreyfus and Taylor adduced this as an alternative to the cartesian mediation theory (Dreyfus & Taylor, 2015). In contrast to the pure physical resonance, for social or vivid resonance, there are three aspects, namely the passive, the active, and the aspect of alienation (Kolb, 2017f). In the mode of genus, we, on the one hand, find the passive one, if we get affected by our sensory perception or prompted by the exchange with other people to gain new knowledge. On the other hand, we can try to influence other ones when swapping ideas with them, so that the active aspect emerges. And if something seems strange to us, the resonance gets damped or falls silent, whereby the aspect of alienation becomes perceptible. In the mode of individuum, the passive aspect, on the one hand, plays a role, if we get seized by our sensations, which also can seem to be strange to us, however, so that the aspect of alienation appears. On the other hand, when judging, we shape resonance actively. In the mode of species, too, all three aspects of resonance arise, the passive one, if our expectations put us in a certain temper, the aspect of alienation, if we meet some difficulties when implementing an intention, and the active one, if we influence our environment.

If we look still more exactly, we must admit that our resonance contact is direct, and my epistemology is a contact theory in this sense, but the praxis with this contact is mediated, namely in the mode of genus by other ones, in the mode if individuum by oneself resp. by one's own impulses or vivid utterances, and in the mode of species by our own skills and dexterities resp. by the effectivity of our activities, that is by our experiences. Insofar by this theory, our knowledge is mediated, too, and there are criteria, we observe in dealing with the direct contact with reality. That there is something, we realize immediately by the contact resp. by the resonance with, what we meet. What it is in each case, we realize by criteria. These are predefined by our culture as common-sense resp. as "sound human understanding", and they are conveyed to us during our education in the first years of our life. That we may challenge these criteria individually anytime and change them, this is the achievement of modern times, which first was philosophically justified by Descartes. This is his merit. But it is useless to question all in all, because for the questioning we already need criteria, and at some point, we must stop questioning, otherwise we do not get around to living and being alive[7]. It is namely an illusion to suppose, we could come to adamant truths eventually, which are uncircumventable.

An epistemology propagating critical questioning should be asked, what for it ought to ask. This is the essential question, the question about the what-for, which Heidegger recognized as first step, before you ask for the Sein itself (Heidegger, 2006a). Before I ask for gaining knowledge, I first must ask, which purpose knowledge ought to fulfill, knowledge for knowledge's sake seems to be absurd. Kant realized this problem as well and consequently separated "is" from "ought", trying to solve the problem by distinguishing the pure from the practical reason. This solution however is too short-sighted and not radical enough, seized the problem not at its roots, because he only asked, "What ought I to do?", instead like Heidegger, "What for ought I to do what?" or "Which kind of concern or for-the-sake-of-which is behind all?", to get by this to the native, unquestionable, uncircumventable, but also inaccessible foundations of all Sein.

---

[7] This we also must convey to our children, who otherwise will not be able to stop asking questions.

By this, it is not only about the concern of one's own realm, about autonomy and self-determination and the dissociation of the public at large, of the "They", as Heidegger calls it. By too much emphasizing the individuum resp. the holistic self-understanding in its total timeliness, he is only about the boundary between inside and outside – here, Heidegger is still entangled in the cartesian image of the world. It is not only about timeliness and understanding of oneself, but also about spatiality resp. about the contact[8] with the strange, to make it familiar, this is the what-for here, namely the communicative solidarity and the autonomy, as Rentsch formulated it (Rentsch, 1999, p. 258). Rentsch also emphasizes the purpose of analyses, which can never be reasonable for their own sake, by writing, an "anthropology cannot be conceptualized prae- or extra-ethical (ibidem, p. I, own translation).

The example of a living cell explains the importance of independence, contact, and purpose: on one side, there is the cell membrane being important for the first, on the other side, the cell makes contact with its surrounding, acquaints itself with all the vibrations of its environment and answers with corresponding frequences. By this, the wave character of its elementary particles is protected, in order that quantum effects, which are necessary for surviving, are possible. Here, the purpose of the cell is to remain alive in its world. Thomas Nagel emphasizes the importance of goals, too, when he rejects the materialist neo-darwinian conception of nature as almost certainly false and suggests a teleological conception instead (Nagel, 2012).

In the cartesian image of the world resp. in the materialist neo-darwinian conception of the world, immediate experiences of contact or resonance are not admitted, because they are inaccessible, i.e. especially, they cannot be repeated as often as needed, the scientific quality criterion of reliability cannot be fulfilled. Immediate experiences of contact only then are not derided, if they lead to ideas or theories, which can be verified or falsified by experiment, so that here knowledge in the scientific

---

[8] Contact comes from Latin contangere, to touch each other, and this is something spatial.

sense can be gained. But on the other hand, in the same culture, they operate with promises of resonance to motivate people to take part in social life. Such discrepancies like e.g. that one between numb experimenting with living beings, animals as well as men, without any resonance, and sneaky technics of advertisement, which for example promise us the resonance experience of a clear conscience, if we use a certain fabric softener (will it soften our brain, too?), for me, these are signs of alienation from our actual reality.

In the Indian culture as a contrast, to explain the general problematic issue, experiences of resonance are highly esteemed as mystic experiences. But instead of looking for criteria, how to classify these experiences to be able to act more effectively in proper life, as scientists here deal with so called brainstorms, each trial to use those immediate experiences practically is discarded as senseless. The only criteria that have been looked for in the Indian culture, have been those, with the help of which you could get as deep mystic experiences as possible and by this a connection to the highest might. These have been gathered in the different directions of Yoga (Yoga indeed means connection). Herein and in everydaylife routines to survive, the practical dealings with being-in-the-world exhaust themselves.

In dealing with immediate experiences of contact and resonance, we find in both cultures, in the Indian and in our western one, tendencies, which foster as well as restrict our capability to love. In the Indian cultural area the capability to love is fostered in the mode of individuum by more and more developing the holistic self-understanding by Yoga, and Buddhism fostered the capability to love in the mode of genus especially in China and Japan, while in the mode of species the autonomous effective acting, the active charity, was deemed useless. Just here, our western culture has achieved enormously much, but activities in both other realms resp. modes were denigrated or even used for manipulation when advertising, or still much more dangerously applied abusively in demagogic actions for one's own egoistic purposes.

The question of getting knowledge can be deepened by considerations of childhood development and of learning theories. However, knowledge differs from learned contents by that knowledge always is explicit, i.e. especially that we can pass it to other ones resp. communicate it. Therefore knowledge exists in form of representations, but this does not mean that representations are the exclusive reasons of all knowledge. Evolutionarily learning starts, because we can detect contingencies, a capability, which we already come to earth with (Fonagy, Gergely, Jurist, & Target, 2004), and which is the same capability of perceiving resonance (Kolb, 2017f). In principle, each type of resonance resp. mirroring is already attractive for a new-borne baby, but there is a remarkable speciality "that after the age of about 3 months, the target setting of the contingency-detection mechanism of the normal human infant is switched toward seeking out high but imperfect [instead of perfect] degrees of contingency" (Fonagy, Gergely, Jurist, & Target, 2004, p. 188), i.e. at the latest, from three months on, the opposite familiar-strange is opened for the infant, and it learns to affectively distinguish pursuant conditions more and more, to sensationally conceive them by means of its own stirrings or impulses, and to apply expectantly feeling, what it has decided, with the aid of its own considerations and evaluations. The learnt contents by this will be changed into knowledge only from the developmental level of the representational self (ibidem), namely from about four years of age.

As mentioned above, there are three sources of knowledge, the communicative exchange with other ones in the being-there mode of genus, one's own stirrings or impulses in the mode of individuum, and the encounter with earthly things in the mode of species, and because the three modes of being-there are in an absolute dialectical relation of conveyance, none of these sources can be preferred. Also, there is no absolute boundary between them, but they blend into each other, the exchange with other ones blends into a change of one's own stirrings or impulses, and these moderate the encounter with earthly things, what in turn influences the exchange with other ones etc.

When understanding is "bound to mediation", as Dreyfus and Taylor call the conceptions, which come from Descartes' philosophy (Dreyfus & Taylor, 2015), there are only two sources of knowledge, on one side, our knowledge is grounded "in the acquisition of previously interpreted data" (ibidem) – let us call this the realm of reasons –, on the other side, it is caused by encountering earthly things – let us call this the realm of causes. Between both sources, there must be an absolute boundary, otherwise we cannot accept, because of the skeptical outlook of this philosophy, that we tolerate the encounter without reasons. Once we have found some reason by interpretation, we can have found this only by further encounters of earthly things, which again we cannot tolerate without reasons either, so that the search for reasons and causes is without any end. When children were told reasons by their parents conveying thus knowledge to them, they use to ask why and want to probe the reasons and causes. Sometimes they would carry things ad infinitum, till their parents put an end to this, because it is useless.

However, an absolute boundary between the realm of reasons and the realm of causes introduces new problems. In the realm of reasons we are absolutely free, critical thinking and interpreting are spontaneously open and free, and in the realm of causes we are absolutely equal. An absolute boundary gainsays our deeply implanted desire for both to be connected, liberty and equality. Kant tried to unite both by the categorical imperative, what, however, could not succeed for that reason alone that here we must manage a problem of relationship, which nobody can solve on his own. The unification of absolute freedom and absolute egality can be accomplished in perfect love only (Kolb, 2017a, p. 247 et seqq.).

These difficulties and unsolvable problems we escape, if we accept the previously mentioned three sources of knowledge, since they are in an absolute dialectical relation of conveyance (two convey the third, and this mediates between those two), so that none of them can be preferred. The realm of reasons is the realm of concepts altogether conveying a Weltanschauung, we can discuss in the mode of genus together with others, and the realm of causes gets open to us in the mode of species meeting something in the world. Both realms convey the realm of our everyday life, which relates both together. As you can easily see, there is an absolute dialectical relation of conveyance between the three realms, so that there is neither an absolute boundary between reasons and causes nor convey reasons alone causes or causes alone reasons. Finally, we thus can realize and explain to us, not only that and how the contents of knowledge are gained, but also that and how they influence and organize themselves.

3. Psychological und Psychoanalytic Concepts and Theories

Since Freud foregrounded the drives and thus the bodily-material aspect by championing the thesis that the neurotic suffers from the reminiscence of unfulfilled drive wishes, and because quite generally all psychoanalytic theories assume a conflict model of psychic disturbances, where our bodiliness plays some role, I shall shine a light on this aspect of being-there first, and on its relation to the other two aspects of the psychic-motivational and the mindful-ideal one, and show up, which meaning the different modes of being-there, genus, individuum, and species, have in connection with the different aspects, namely what is individual, specific or general for the bodily, psychic, and mindful aspect in each case.

Further I shall show based on the development of a child, as presented by Fonagy (Fonagy, Gergely, Jurist, & Target, 2004), how the being-there modes, the being-there aspects, and the being-there structures develop, and demonstrate, when a child can discover the ontological difference between appearance of some concrete being (German "Seiendes") we meet and underlying being (German "Sein") resp. underlying existence. Coherences between capability to love, superego formation, and sublimation, as well as being-there-analytic considerations, what consciousness, unconscious and dreaming mean, plus analyses of basic levels of language and experience round out this chapter, after previously I have analyzed the different emotions, which on the developmental level of the sexual self resp. , as defined in "Dasein, um zu lieben" (Kolb, 2017a) and in "Liebe, Macht und Sexualität" (Kolb, 2017c), become more and more important.

3.1. Body, Psyche, and Mind

As concepts the aspects of the bodily, the psychic, and the mindful – or shortly body, psyche, and mind – are imaginations resp. representations of reality or of parts of it, and as such not derivable from reality, but only from practical life, from our dealings with the reality of life, namely from, if and how far our imaginations are useful in practical life, whereby useful means that by these we are deluded resp. disappointed as little as possible. Thus first, the question arises, how these concepts are used in everyday life, what is their meaning in everyday language (the meaning indeed is their use according to Wittgenstein), and what does this tell about us and our understanding of ourselves and others.

The German word for mind is "Geist" and can be translated with spirit and ghost, too. So, if I speak of mind, I also mean spirit and ghost. Wittgenstein means, we talk about a mind/spirit/ghost (I think, he means a non-bodily imagined entity, often with humanlike features and supernatural capabilities), where we suppose something, but where there is nothing. "Where our language lets us suppose a body, and there is no body, there, we might say, would be a spirit." (§ 36, own translation) (Wittgenstein, 2001) If by a man we expect a brain (this is bodily, too) with much intelligence, but must ascertain that there is nothing, at least no brain with much intelligence, this does not mean that this man is very spirited – here mind/spirit/ghost blanketly denotes all cognitive abilities of men. But it may be that we shudder and are seized and excited, what corresponds to the Indo-Germanic root "gheis-" (viz. ghost and German Geist). The ancestral spirit can blow in certain masonries – this reminds of the Greek "pneuma", wind or breath. The spirit of the French Revolution kept the whole of Europe in suspense, so that they hardly could breath. The spirit in alcoholic beverages, by the effect of which we suppose something, what we cannot see, only smell, can impair our spirit in the sense of our ability to think. Cavell says, he has "spoken of there being a spirit in which words may be meant" (Cavell, 1979, p. 379). Here mind/spirit/ghost is a characteristic of a language community and reminds of the "objective spirit" of Hegel, which gets manifested in communities, as this concept is also used in Max Weber's speech of the "Spirit of Capitalism".

Mind/spirit/ghost is thus something individual in language use, if I talk about mine and, what I think and mean, it is something specific, if I mean my cognitive capabilities and dexteries, and it is something general, if it confronts a community that is oriented towards it. Since as orientation it targets a direction and thus points to something higher (and in Christianity unites all men as the Holy Ghost, so that they will find back to God), you may denote it as the aspect of return to perfect love (see 2.2). It is also interesting that "Geist" in German grammar is male, and this corresponds to the male commander, the so called task leader in social psychology, who protects a community against dangers from outside and cares for resources from the environment.

By contrast, psyche is female in German grammar, and as a soul is *in* a community – unlike spirit, which is *above* or *opposite* a community – it corresponds to the so called social emotional leader in social psychology, which cares for harmony inside a community and that everybody feels as good as possible. The soul is the characteristic of all living beings and thus a symbol for vivid dynamic and for life altogether; and what makes men and animals alive, are the sensations resp. the sensational state of mind, because they constitute the relation to each of their being-in-the-world. Insofar psyche and soul are used synonymous. In contrast to the spirit, which strives upward, the soul is profound. It is so, "as though it is an unbreachable point grammar that a soul is at least as high in the scale of being as the body it happens inhabit. The soul may go beneath itself, but never above; it can only be dragged down." (Cavell, 1979, p. 380) In fairy tales e.g., a human soul never slips into a higher being like a fairy or an angel, but only into animals, plants, or even things. Words are meant in a certain spirit and can express something from the soul. In language use, a soul is something individual, if I mean my own vividness and sensations, it is something specific, if it gives me power and motivation to execute some plan or action, and it is something general, it creates common values in a community, so that they have a common agenda. Altogether, the soul supplies with the power, in order that the return to perfect love, predetermined by the spirit, can be performed. Therefore, I denoted the soul resp. the psyche as the aspect of the dynamic of perfect love (see 2.2).

By this, it becomes obvious that mind/spirit and psyche/soul must work together, in order that the being-there develops in the direction towards perfect love. In its profoundness the soul goes down to the least being and thus absorbs all forces to get to love. In the Greek mythology the profoundness of the soul is expressed by that it goes down into the underworld after death, the same reason why Jesus first went down to hell after his death, too. If we imagine soul and spirit like woman and man, then in the context that the soul profoundly coalesces with the realm of the dead and death, and that the spirit tends upward to God and to the origin of life, the following imagination is fitting: in orgasm women experience a dedication like when dying, while men regress to the "most primitive level of object relations" (Balint, 1988, p. 128, own translation), i.e. to the most primordial level of existence, as it prevailed at the beginning of his life, of his primordial unavailability. In orgasm the women connect with death, and the men strive upward to the beginning of all life. What happens with men in orgasm, is quite good described by Balint (ibidem), while the orgasm of women is presented in the myth of Persephone and Hades as death for example. The Celtic myth of Harlekin interpretes the death as ultimative orgasm of women, too (McClelland, 2006). You can put it like this: men in orgasm strive for the divine origin of life, while women in orgasm dedicate themselves to death and by this to their mortality. When both gets connected, begin and end of life, man and woman, spirit and soul, then a zygote can be animated. Thus, a space arises, which is limited by the laws of begin and end, the rhythm of life. Fitting to that, it is said by Jaucourt: "[…] rhythm is nothing else, but a space limited by certain laws." (Naumann, 2005, p. 50, own translation)

The human body presents the material aspect of men. About its relation to psyche/soul and mind/spirit, there are corresponding myths and developmental stories. Imprinting for our Christian culture is the biblical creation story: the body as a mass of clay is ensouled and at the same time inspired by the breath of God, and by the Fall of Man, when Adam and Eve ate from the tree of knowledge – here the body and the material come into play, to which the doubt, *embodied* by the snake, has attributed a false function, namely that the material can convey the same like God, and that it can make Adam and Eve happy – this primordial soul-spirit (the breath of God) was devided into that, what today we call soul and spirit.

If the body and the material are absolutized, psyche and mind get into a growing contrast and dissent. This rupture or segregation of mind/spirit and psyche/soul is the origin of the evil resp. of sin, the original sin, because this seperation of mind and psyche was inherited on and on. Here, man has separated, what has been one from God. To match both to the divine soul-spirit, is our task, we can solve only "in the sweat of our face", that is only by means of our material-bodily basis, which we ought to give its true meaning, and which shows us again and again with merciless openness, what point we just are at concerning our development resp. how much soul and spirit are still separated and contrary.

Since mind is male and psyche female (see above), if you look at it that way, it is about the emancipated unification of man and woman. When Heideger speaks of sensational understanding and Wittgenstein views language not only as a tool of the transmission of thoughts, but also as an expression of sensations, then you can see in this the same tendency, namely the attempt to establish this unification of mind and psyche, which is possible according to my analysis only in the true and immediate understanding of the for-the-sake-of-which of our being, thus only in perfect love. As long as soul and spirit are still in contrast, the human body reveals the corresponding opposites and presents by this the alienation of love (see 2.2).

In this myth of Adam and Eve resp. in this imagination, the human body is the mediating element between soul and spirit, by means of which they can find to each other, after they have been primordially separated by the absolutizing of the body. This developmental history fits in with Wittgenstein´s imagination that the "human body [is] the best picture of the human soul[/spirit]" (Wittgenstein, 2001, p. 1002, PU 496, own translation). The human body is individual, insofar as I can perceive it as my own, it is specific, insofar as it has developed in a certain way and goes on developing with certain capabilities and dexteries, each of which arise and vanish, and it is general, insofar as it is built by the same atoms and molecules, is realized by all as human body, and can express something mindful or psychic in similar ways.

As long as I conceive my bodiliness as mediating element between the psychic and the mindful and find my bearings by my bodily perceivable self-concern such that I watch out for the harmony of psyche/soul and mind/spirit and strive for the unity of both, I am in my rhythm where the modes of genus, individuum, and species recur in a similar way and alternate. Then, I am on the way to perfect love.

The two main manners of perceiving our body as constellation of parts and as vivid wholeness – vivid means that we assume that this wholeness has a relationship to its being-in-the-world – I denoted as gross and subtle or as rough- and fine-material (Kolb, 2017b). These aspects resp. structures of the human body, the gross and the subtle resp. corpus and body (Schmitz, 2011, denoted it as "Körper und Leib") only concern how we perceive matter, namely if we use a grid and according to this break down the perceived into independent parts, the constellation of which we then analyze as far as possible without any sensations, or if we leave the perceived as a whole and respond to certain stimuli of reference, each of which we assign a vivid gestalt taken from our memory, i.e. a gestalt with a relation to its being-in-the-world, such that we can conceive as encompassing as possible our affects resp. our concern triggered by perceiving resp. distinguishing, so that these affects change into a sensation of self-concern.

When conceiving our bodiliness as mediating element between the psychic and the mindful, I previously have perceived my body as something subtle or fine-material, certain references show me the vivid gestalts of my soul/psyche and my spirit/mind, and only by this I intuitively can conceive my body as a reflection of psyche and mind plus their relation to each other.

But the human body still shows another feature, we up to now still have not observed: we can distinguish female and male bodies the same way as on the level of individual outlooks there are the male and the female principle, each of which gets more and more manifested on the developmental level of the sexual self (Kolb, 2017b). The female principle that it is necessary to dedicate one's own concerns and first to help others, this is figuratively spoken first to descend to those not so far developed to help themselves, corresponds more to the soul/psyche, steadily and dynamically engaged in reaching perfect love, while the male principle that it is necessary first to consolidate the own position, before you support others, figuratively spoken first to ascend to corresponding high capabilities and capacities, so that then you can really and much more effectively help, expresses more the outlook of the spirit/mind striving to find back to perfect love.

When Eve is created out of a rib of Adam[9] in the myth of Adam and Eve, this may be interpreted like this: Adam was built up out of clay, which had to be enobled by God's breath, while Eve from her basic substance already was noble and only had to be formed correspondingly. Adam with his male body had come from down the earth and strived up to the divine, while Eve came from above, from the divine idea that being alone is not good for Adam, and thus strived down for the dynamic support of Adam. Insofar Adam embodies the mindful/spiritual and Eve the psychic/emotional. Both have been bodily united in the beginning, but then became estranged from each other by doubts embodied by the snake, as the progress of the myth shows.

If now, you only concentrate on the evil, symbolized in the myth of Adam and Eve by the snake, whereby this means on the one hand the snaking hair and thus the beauty of Eve, which she is smug about, namely to be as irresistible as God, and on the other hand Adam's flash of inspiration snaking from above that he could be as mighty as God, then you could come up with the idea of only having to disguise Eve's beauty and her hair by wearing a headscarf as sometimes demanded in Islam. But then consequently, you should require all men to humbly cover or veil any and all status and potency symbols. Such ideas are intelligable

---

[9] The Hebrew word "tsäla" may be translated as rib or as side resp. aspect, and this means that Eve was formed out of an aspect of Adam and then put on his side. So, Adam and Eve own common and different aspects side by side.

and led by the good intention to eliminate the evil, but they fall short insofar as they do not change anything concerning the ignorance of men, which it is dependent of that a passionate impulse of volition arises, so that psyche or mind are doubted and by this the evil gets manifested in matter. Such a manifestation cannot be prevented by veiling, suppressing or denying.

Cavell cooked up a totally different myth in contrast to the story of Adam and Eve (Cavell, 1979, p. 380 et seqq.) concerning the developmental history of our body: human beings might have been bodiless beings primordially, who had taken their pick of certain guises, human guises, which they had been slipped in, partly out of sheer fun, partly because they had benefitted from that. In the beginning they could change the body, the guise, anytime, only when they had taken a guise too long, then they could not change the guise except by the death of the body. Meanwhile the trick to slip into guises had gone and everybody would be bound to his body lifelong.

Without a human being the human guise would be a zombie, but you could not distinguish this from a man in human guise, unless you opened the body checked up. However, nature had built such a body shell that nobody could distinguish a human guise and a human being. "The shell became skin thin, and when you would open it up you found no separate human being but merely what you would expect to find if you opened an old-fashioned, unshelled human being." (ibidem, p. 380, f.) Since the knowledge of these occurrences has been forgotten, "it even seems hard [...] to imagine how we were fortunate enough ever to have formed the idea of the one inside, grasped the truth of the matter." (ibidem, p. 381) And if today men say, there is nobody inside the body, "this only keeps alive the impulse to look. [(passage)] Is it that we take ourselves for (possibly) inhabited bodies, human beings in undiscardable human guise?" (ibidem) Thus the human body seems to be an obstacle hiding from view, what goes on inside a human being.

Thus, this myth floats an imagination of the human body, which discourages us and stops our motivation to overcome our being-separated from other ones. When accepting this imagination, we are hopelessly separated from ourselves, too: "I cannot lay hands on myself any more intimately than you can. And memory here would be a thin reed. None of us remembers our birth though each of us knows that he or she is natal, so to speak. Do we not?" (ibidem) Our body is estranged from ourselves, we appropriate it like a piece of clothing, and it obstructs the possibilities to us to recognize the other one as well as ourselves. "This again takes the problem of other minds to be of a familiar epistemological form, the form bequeathed by Kant, following Locke and Leibniz, according to which I am sealed within my circle of experiences, never (under my own power) to know whether those experiences match an independent reality." (ibidem, p. 381, f.)

When I apply this imagination in relation to myself, then "I want to escape this body not, pretty clearly, in order to compare (or rather correlate) the responses it shows with the responses I have [...] but simply to reveal my responses. But why should I want this, want it perhaps enough to die for it by leaving my body?" (ibidem, p. 382) If Cavell supposes at this point that maybe it is about getting recognized resp. acknowledged, about getting a confirmation of "the existence of my suffering and of my deeds" (ibidem), then I only must take the position of a physically or sexually abused child, and everything perfectly fits together. If nobody believes me as a thus misused child, it is the rule that "I fail to believe in my expression of myself, my capacity to be able to present myself for acknowledgement" (ibidem). From this perspective I give up and make no more utterances by saying to myself: "There is a very good reason not to do so. You may discover that you do not matter." (ibidem, p. 383)

If we look at the whole myth of Cavell once more from the perspective of an abuse, then the story is told, how this may happen. The offender, a grown-up man, uses a human body, namely an unprotected child, to have fun with it. Doing this he often thinks the child a numb being, a zombie, that does not know anything afterwards and that does not matter. The longer he does so, the worse the consequences until the child is hopelessly trapped and prefers to die to escape the whole thing. "The one inside suffers everything that happens to the body, and more besides." (ibidem, p. 381) (A crueler interpretation would be that the offender, if he has abused the child too long, fears to get convicted by the child or dependent from the child in some other way, and therefore he kills the child.)

When the child becomes grown-up, the times of abuse are long gone, but all "who are now inside human guises are stuck inside for life" (ibidem, p. 380), they lifelong must live with this horrible experience, even if there is lack of any evidence and the experience is separated or suppressed. But though they say or "like to say [...] "There is no one inside" [, ...] this only keeps alive the impulse to look." (ibidem) To come to terms with the traumatic abuse, it is not enough merely to acknowledge "how it is with you, and hence acknowledge that you want the other to care, at least to care to know. It is equally to acknowledge that your expressions in fact express you, that they are yours, that you are in them. This means allowing yourself to be comprehended, something you can always deny. Not to deny it is, I would like to say, to acknowledge your body, and the body of your expressions, to be yours, you on earth, all there will ever be of you." (ibidem, p. 383) So if the body is sensed as an obstacle to recognize men (oneself or others), this can be an indication that the person in concern has been physically or sexually abused resp. has testified this, when it happened to another person.

Deeming my body an obstacle I perceive it grossly or rough-materially as a constellation of particles I have broken it to or it has been broken to. But then, basically not my body but the grid, used to crack it, is the obstacle. It is no different case than with a mirror: while it is whole, I can see myself in it, but if it is broken to pieces, my picture is distorted, and I can no more recognize me the right way. If it seems to me that my body is an obstacle, then my rhythm is disturbed resp. I am thrown out of my rhythm, because the rhythmical process, where I run through the three modes of genus, individuum, and species again and again, is interrupted resp. hindered, in fact at that point, when I change from the mode of species to the one of genus, since here comes the moment, where I would normally perceive, which results I have obtained by my acting as species. If then my body is an obstacle to recognize my soul/psyche and my spirit/mind, I cannot compare these action results with my mindful expectations related to my psychic seizedness, and thus I cannot conceive, whether and how far I have deluded myself. Whatever I do, I no more can feel myself as a part of a community, my physically or sexually abused body prevents the transition from the mode of species to the one of genus and to talk about my horrible experiences to others.

Now, let us come back to the alternative imagination that the body is the best picture of the human soul, resp. that our relation to or our imagination of the body shows us, which conflicts between soul/psyche and mind/spirit have not yet been solved. This conflict of recognizing human beings, the conflict made clear to us by the reference to our body, if we sense it as an obstacle, we can outline this conflict such that our soul wants to be understood, while our spirit is suppressing this. Reasons for each position of soul/psyche and spirit/mind are described above, and possibilities to solve this conflict have been suggested, at least roughly.

What kind of conflict becomes clear, if somebody thinks his body is his own or even in thrall to him, if it is very important to him "that one's body should not be subject to an alien will" (ibidem, p. 383), even if from owning it does not stringently follow "that one's body should be subject to one's own will" (ibidem)? Here in my opinion, it is about a striving for power, which springs either from the spirit or from the soul and thus provokes a conflict between both; "any performance or deed can be done through will or through grace" (ibidem, p. 384), that is through will to power or through striving for harmony (grace). If there is a will, then soul and spirit are in conflict and you will get some slub only, but if soul and spirit work together in harmony, then everything is slick and by this artwork.

When soul/psyche and spirit/mind are in harmony, then there is nothing left to lose, because we own everything and nothing, and thus we are really free. If in terms of Kant an imperative is technically useful or hypothetically pleasant (Kant, Grundlegung zur Metaphysik der Sitten, 1785 (A), zweite Auflage 1786 (B)), then either the spirit or the soul is dominating. Only if the imperative is categorical, soul and spirit are in balance. Thus, it becomes clear that Kant's categorical imperative, the Taoist wu wei (unintentional doing), the absolute harmony resp. unity of spirit and soul, the true and immediate understanding of the for-the-sake-of-which of our being, that is perfect love, and the absolute nothing (see 2.2) altogether amount to the same thing.

Our bodiliness becomes apparent not only to ourselves, but we also express it by different cultural products, i.e. by dummies, statues and robots, which partly show our bodiliness, partly take over its functions: shop window dummies show, how clothes may look on us, statues remind us of certain personages and maybe advise or warn us, and robots and machines take over certain operations and thus replace our body. We have certain dealings with dummies or dollies, we play with e.g., with statues, we put on a platform, and with robots and machines, we construct and build. But what conclusions can we draw about, how we partly deal with ourselves and with others?

This complex of themes I explicitly have dealt with in "Gedanken zu Stanley Cavells „Der Anspruch der Vernunft""" (Kolb, 2012b), so that here I can be brief: for me the essential conclusion, I have drawn from what I have shown up there about dummies, statues, and robots, is that because of the absolute dialectical relation of conveyance (see 2.1) neither the psychic-motivational nor the mindful-idealistic nor the bodily-material, meaning neither soul nor spirit nor body have any preference concerning our being human, but that we again and again have a tendency to overestimate one of them and give too little value to the other aspects of our being human.

If we overestimate our body, we deck ourselves or our children out like dolls, narcissistically pay attention only to external beauty we never reach, however, so that we fare badly like Tantalos, who sacrificed his (inner and his actual) child to the Gods – so do we, if we make ourselves or our children dollies – and whose penalty, the torments of Tantalos, was that he saw all the joys of life around himself, but could not reach them, when he tried to seize them, and this being-separated creates **hopelessness** and suffering.

With the idolization of external beauty, we deny its evanescence and death. If, however, we denigrate our body, this brings us into the position, where we must prove that we are in some way exceptional and outstanding from the aspect of either psyche or mind, meaning good and not evil or clever and not stupid. In the second case we fixate on something, become rigid like a statue, continuously must document our progress, try to outwit the boundaries of our life, and become slaves of progress, which we, like Sisyphos, who outsmarted death, like a heavy stone again and again must heave up on the (achievement) summit of a mountain, which again and again it will roll down from. This way typically, men use to act, if they have assumed the traditional male role, with the feeling of **overextension** resp. rage. In the first case, if we want to prove that we are good according to the psychic-motivational, what corresponds to the traditional female role, we develop a helping syndrome, i.e. we care for others and forget our own wishes, needs and belongings, so that earlier or later we feel more and more **helpless** and thus anxious.

As an illustration of the two latter attitudes the following story may serve: A spiritual teacher asks three of his pupils, what they would do, if they found a wallet full of money in the street. When the first answered, "I would do everything, in order that the legitimate owner would get back his wallet", the teacher said to him: "You hypocrite!" When the second answered, he of course would keep the wallet for himself, the teacher said to him: "You villain!" But when the third answered, he would entreat God to give him the power to do the right thing and to return the wallet to the legitimate owner, the teacher said: "This is the right attitude, if you know your psychic, mindful, and bodily deficiencies, but do not indulge, neither from the soul, nor from the spirit, nor from the body."

The hypocrite resp. the idealist pays attention to his moral impact by believing he must prove he is good and not evil/bad, overestimates the psychic-motivational und the purity of the soul and thinks this the most important like a dogmatist. The villain resp. the materialist wants to prove he is clever and not stupid, he overestimates the mind by this and believes he can satisfy his material needs with prudent and reasonable thinking and acting only, and does not need to pay attention to anything else, and only the third pupil knows about the deficiencies of body, mind and soul, estimates all of them equal, uses all of them to do the right thing: To entreat God means to unite soul/psyche and spirit/mind (God's breath indeed was the unity of soul and spirit he made Adam alive with), so that the self is not disrupted, but forms a union to be able to give the right direction to the power and energy of his body for the corresponding deed.

Body, spirit, and soul must be seen together as different aspects of a human being, if we want to understand being human better and better. If we loved perfectly, that is if we had reached the utopian goal to truly and immediately understand the for-the-sake-of-which of all being, then we would see the aspect of alienation from perfect love in the body, the aspect of return to perfect love in the spirit/mind, and the dynamic aspect of perfect love in the soul/psyche, so that body, spirit, and soul would be realized as a union. Vice versa, the more you can see body, spirit, and soul together as a union, the more you understand the dynamic in the psychic, the giving direction in the mindful, and the vividly showing the relation of spirit and soul in the bodiliness, if and how far soul and spirit still are estranged from each other. This perception resp. differentiation can only be subtle resp. fine-material. To reach more and more harmony, familiarity, and union between spirit and soul and thus in the bodiliness, too, you more and more need the true and immediate understanding of the for-the-sake-of-which of one's own and the being of all others, since the own being-there is a being-in-the-world and therefore interrelates with every other being. So, we more and more need perfect love, and when striving for harmony, familiarity, and union between the aspects of spirit and soul, we more and more develop in the direction of perfect love, and this provides our bodily wellness, too, so that we have an important criterion for the fact, whether we really move into the right direction.

3.2. Developmental Aspects of Being-There

At this point I only want to recapitulate, what earlier I already have described in my three books (Kolb, 2017a; Kolb,

2017b; Kolb, 2017c) much more explicitly about the development of children from the viewpoint of being-there analysis.

Right after birth infants are only an extension of their mothers and rudimentarily developed only in the mode of genus as objects of matter (sensual-affective perception) and psychic subjects (innate contingency-detection module), the remaining functions in the mode of genus and those in the other two modes their mothers must assume for them entirely. In general, the whole development is only possible with the help of the mother or another important caregiver, a human being is never growing up on its own.

On the level of the physical self, infants as psychic subjects in the mode of genus develop a communication level together with their mother with the help of their contingency-detection module, and first functions in the other two modes of individuum and species. There is already a first differentiation, especially by the emotions, which they sense as objects of the psyche and feel as objects of the mindful spirit because of the rudimentarily conceived affect of fascination. Sensations of joy (individual), which motivate to repeat activities, and concretely inviting expectations and feelings of fun (specific) can be identified and thus as objects of their mind the presence or absence of a prompting or an order resp. the opposite active-passive or own determination of their environment vs. the one of their mothers. Furthermore, you can already realize the three aspects psyche, mind, and matter. Concerning the structures of being-there, there are already beginnings of vivid reality and spatiality, and concerning timeliness the actual moment, and for this structure only partly the ecstasy of arrival, time is only a mere joining together of meaningful points of time without any further coherence.

During the subsequent progress the communication gets more and more differentiated and its functions more and more diverse, until finally the human language and thus the full spectrum of human possibilities of communication are developed. The differentiation of affects, sensations, and feelings and their possibilities of regulation increase further, so that finally

1. flare/reluctance (general affect), anger/distaste (individual sensation), and rage/revulsion (specific feeling) emerge in reaction to a *hardship situation*, which the being-there as psychic subject has affectively seizing understood as such, this altogether in the context of the accordingly understood oppositeness *objective-subjective* on the developmental level of the *social* self,

2. shock (general affect), anxiety (individual sensation) and fear (specific feeling) in reaction to a situation of *helplessness*, which the being-there as psychic subject has affectively seizing understood as such, this altogether in the context of the accordingly understood oppositeness *continuous-discontinuous* on the developmental level of the *teleological* self,

3. pain (general affect), suffering (individual sensation) and grief (specific feeling) in reaction to a situation of *hopelessness*, which the being-there as psychic subject has affectively seizing understood as such, this altogether in the context of the accordingly understood oppositeness *linear-circular* on the developmental level of the *intentional* self,

4. and consternation (a mixture of the previous general negative affects), disappointment resp. shame (individual sensation) and indignation resp. guilt feelings (specific feelings) in reaction to a situation of first other one´s *deficiency* (capability to be guilty for Heidegger), which the being-there as psychic subject has affectively seizing understood as such, and finally of one´s own deficiency and of the too big responsibility, this altogether in the context of the accordingly understood oppositeness *spatial-temporal* on the developmental level of the *representational* self.

We can more exactly realize the *aspect of the psyche* as the dynamic-sensual one, i.e. affectively seizing understanding of conditionality resulting from the reprocessing of previous experiences (even from others) meaning from the dynamic relation between the action as bodily-material subject and its result perceived as object of matter, further, more exactly realize the *aspect of the mind* as the sensually expectantly understanding of the possibilities of the capability to be because of previous experiences (of others as well), and finally, more exactly realize the *aspect of matter* as the practical understanding of difficulties, when we err in dealing with the kinds of oppositeness above concerning the expectations of our mind, so that we overcome each delusion and the resulting sensation of disappointment decisively and persistently. For this the *support and help* of the mother is not only important concerning the *regulation of the* corresponding *emotions*, the (spatial) overabundance of the general sensational-affective stimuli, the (rhythmical) excitement of the individual sensational self-concern, and the (temporal) strain of the specific felt expectations, meaning altogether the corresponding affectively busy perceptional basis of anger/distaste, anxiety, suffering, and disappointment resp. shame as well as of the corresponding feelings, but she is prompting her children on and on to *change perspective* to understand the aspects of the vivid reality negating each other, namely the just mentioned kinds of oppositeness of matter, better and better and by this to overcome their oppositeness more and more.

If we look at the development of children from the level of the psychic self to the one of the representational self, then their Weltanschauung, how something appears to them, is different on each level. Thus, there is a certain plurality of worlds of appearances, and the question arises, how children get from one phenomenal world to the next one. Up to now we mainly looked at the part of mothers, who supported such transitions by calming and by inducing changes of perspectives. But what are the preconditions for the children, which developmental processes are required in order that they can use the support of their mothers, so that a new world becomes accessible to them?

With each of the five developmental levels a pair of opposites is connected as a material anchoring. Only after children succeed up to a certain degree to deal with the corresponding opposites, meaning with the material level, by practical acting, the next developmental level becomes accessible and thus the corresponding world of appearances, too. Here children can distinguish or perceive still more circumstances, i.e. their world of appearances enlarges more and more, more and more appears to them in this world. The more *insight* into the interdependence between activity and passivity children have on the level of the physical self, the more it occurs to them that their subjective resp. subject-sided effectivity depends on objective resp. object-sided conditions – at first of other people, then of its total environment. By this the level of the social self gets accessible to them. The more they can *regard* such conditions, the more it becomes clear to them that they can continuously string together different specific activities, where the result of a previous activity is the condition for the next, so that they can get to the level of the teleological self. The more *cautiously* they can string together their specific chains of activities, the more they can get the view that they reach certain intentions by this, but sometimes it turns out to be a circle where they must start anew. This gives them the access to the level of the intentional self. The better they can judge their *prospects* and can develop corresponding strategies and thus reach their goals more and more often, the more often they will be confronted with that they have taken other ones the space for possibilities and by time they may be judged more and more negative. As soon as they realize this danger (to get isolated), the level of the representational self is accessible to them, and they are prompted to act with more *circumspect*. To develop this circumspect more and more is an important precondition for the entrance into the life of a grown-up, where they will be confronted with the oppositeness male-female.

As you can see by these presentations, children first need certain experiences, capabilities, and capacities earned by performing their life, before they can enter a new world of appearances. For the transition from one phenomenal world to another one, children do not simply only learn a new interpretation of their perceptions, but they work through certain new experiences, by which they realize that their perspective up to now is not sufficient any more to avoid certain delusions and disappointments. By new perspectives they realize new differences, can differentiate more, and can thus perceive more, namely things as well as properties as well as processes.

Our way of viewing the world on the one hand depends on which different perspectives we take in (mindful aspect), on the other hand we also need certain experiences, which make us attentive and sensible for differences resp. kinds of oppositeness (material aspect), which we can perceive only by means of certain capabilities and capacities to be principally able to distinguish certain perspectives resp. to take them over, and for each change of perspectives we ought not to be too excited (psychic aspect). How the world appears to us, depends on psychic as well as on material as well as on mindful factors. It is not the result of different interpretations of our perception, our perception itself changes, because new differentiations become accessible for us.

Important to mention at this point seems to me that by these considerations I need neither a thing in itself (Kant, Critik der reinen Vernunft, 1781 (A), zweite Auflage 1787 (B)) and derived from this a world in itself, nor any kind of realism where I must assume that some empirical data will help me to describe an objective reality approximately better and better. This comes from that the different phenomenal worlds appear to one and the same child, who by this is better and better getting along with the world. Also, there is no danger of solipsism, because children share all their phenomenal worlds with their mother. (As a mathematician this reminds me of Cauchy's criterion for convergence of sequences and series where you need not know the actual limit.)

In this sense to be able to compare two phenomenal worlds, I need (preferably several) men, who have been in both worlds. Of course, there must be some material anchoring resp. a corresponding criterion, how well somebody has empathized with a phenomenal world: the more I can reproduce similar expectations (imitated development of expectations) like others in the corresponding phenomenal world, and the more I can imagine (imitated perception) similar congruencies and deviations between expectations and actual outcomes, the better or more I can empathize with this phenomenal world. The regarding imitation is most successful, if I myself have practically acted together with other ones in the corresponding world for some time. Mothers learn and understand the phenomenal world of their children that way.

Insofar also a psychotherapist can best conceive an anxious or depressive client and understand how to plan possible ways out of the psychic disturbance, who himself has experienced anxieties and depressions resp. has practically acted under such circumstances. For each kind of empathizing however, it is valid that this is even more successful, the more the person in concern has neared perfect love. For each single one it is valid that he or she can succeed more and more on this way to perfect love and can distinguish resp. perceive this, but she or he can never know, how far away she or he is from there. And if you compare different people, you can never say, who is nearer to perfect love. In the end this is the statement of "before God all men are equal" (Roman 2,11; Ephesian 6,9). How well somebody can empathize with the phenomenal world of somebody else or with the one of a strange community, this can ultimately be measured only by how far and how often he or she is deceived when giving concrete statements of how somebody would practically act in the corresponding phenomenal world in a certain situation.

In how far can you compare people anyway, and is the described development of being-there in the mother-child-dyad not too specific and therefore not applicable to all men in all cultures? On the one hand it is right that here I have drawn an ideal-typical development, which that way (I am sorry) does not always take place even in our own culture. But decisive for the being-there analysis are the different sensations, where for each one it is testified that the being-there wants to overcome the oppositeness connected with it and thus altogether reach perfect love in the end (see 2.2).

The different kinds of oppositeness are universal – developmentally up to the oppositeness linear-circular even universal for many animals – and the different situational characteristics like a successful own determination of one´s environment, over-exerting hardship, helplessness, hopelessness, and deficiencies as well. From these develop the corresponding sensations by all men, which prompt the overcoming of the corresponding kinds of oppositeness: if the own determination of the environment is successful, this elicits joy by everybody and the active striving for more successful determination and no more having to passively tolerate something (overcoming the oppositeness active-passive), and if this is unsuccessful, everybody is frustrated and senses a negative mood. Thereby overexerting hardship makes you angry, helplessness anxious, hopelessness creates suffering, and deficiencies shame or disappointment resp. shame for other ones depending on the attributing of causes, if somebody else or you yourself are perceived as deficient.

Insofar there is a common base, coming from which you can compare all men on the level of sensations, i.e. the aspect of the psychic-motivational is equal for all men. If now you can conceive either the mindful-idealistic or the distinguishable-material aspect in the different situations of everyday-life, then the phenomenal world of the person in concern gets open for you, because between the three aspects psyche, mind, and matter, there is indeed an absolute conveyance.

A further consequence from the considerations of the development of children is the plurality of phenomenal worlds for children on the different developmental levels, which cannot be reduced to a different interpretation of the appearances made by the children, but which also come from an increase of the perceived phenomena because of more capabilities and capacities, they have appropriated by different learning processes. In my opinion you may generalize this for all men, since these different learning processes by common insight, regard, precaution, prospect, and circumspect are generally human, so that hereby is shown "that regarding these subject-sided moments of phenomenal worlds there is a certain space for possibilities, so that different phenomenal worlds result from a variation of subject-sided moments" (Hoyningen-Huene, 1989, p. 74, own translation), and by this the philosophy of science by Kuhn significantly gains more importance (ibidem).

3.3. The Role of Language and Thinking

Next, I want to clear, what exactly is meant by the concepts of "language", "to speak", "to talk", "to think". As described by Hartmann (Hartmann, 1998, p. 164 et seqq.), to speak is using a language, either a performing of plans on the level of the intentional self or a human acting, which expresses something on the level of the representational self. In contrast to this, to talk is speaking with one's voice or by whispering. A language develops from the communication of infants with their mother, who contingently reacts to the stirrings or impulses of her infants, so that her infants detect this contingency and learn thus in certain situations to pursue certain specific activities, which are operantly reinforced by contingent reactions of the mother.

This communication is inter-existential, it is not developed by one alone, what you can realize by that it is distinguishable by the same mother with different of her infants. Since many specific activities of children are accompanied by voice, from this communication the talking develops, unless they are mute. Their mother tongue children first start to learn on the level of the intentional self, where by this way of speaking resp. of talking only signs resp. words as signs are used for the corresponding intentions of the children, and where they understand their mother only on this level of speaking, namely her actions and speaking as signs of her intentions. To understand somebody else here means to imagine you are the other one and understand yourself as the other one. To understand oneself is the same as to develop one or several plans and to imagine possibilities what and how one can be to reach certain own intentions. The understanding of somebody else or of oneself is limited to intentions on this developmental level, which children can distinguish by certain performances of different plans.

Language thus encompasses on this level all activities, which are performances of plans for a child. This also corresponds to the everyday-life use, when we say that a certain activity reveals an intention (to reveal also is a kind of speaking). Looked at it this way, communication is well-founded by that each one of the communicating partners imagines to be the other (sometimes they get the same rhythm of breathing by that after a while), and speaking arises, when the activities of both partners are realized at least as performances of plans, unless even as temporally and spatially relatively independent expressions of the acting one, ac-tivities, which represent a certain peculiarity of him or her resp. which characterize her or him. The latter I want to call an entirely developed human language, because a language like one that a child can develop on the level of the intentional self, this you can also find by animals.

Let us now come to the concept of thinking: Hartmann (ibidem) defines thinking as imagined speaking, what I want to specify that way as imagined speaking-to-each-other. You could also define thinking as imagined communicating, but then you had the difficulty to ascertain, when somebody is thinking or rather has been thinking, because the possibilities of telling, if you have been thinking, are too much limited for this reason, if a child has not yet reached the level of the intentional self and therefore cannot tell having imagined communicating with somebody. Therefore, the definition chosen by Hartmann makes sense, and we can even distinguish between animalistic and entirely devel-oped human thinking as I shall show. Since animals cannot reach the level of the representational self, they cannot speak an en-tirely developed human language, and therefore they cannot im-agine this human speaking, i.e. they cannot think like human be-ings.

The difference between the two ways of thinking can be explained by the two concepts of the sign and the symbol: by a sign its use up to now will be kept, and a sign only can point to something, whereas by a symbol you totally discard its former use and give it a new meaning. When Heidegger´s Southern Baden peasant views the south wind as a sign for coming rain, he still uses the concept of the wind the same way. But if you apply the sea as a symbol for birth, life and death, you totally ignore the use of this concept as salty water, we find at the coasts of our conti-nents. This is a creative process, which however does not proceed arbitrarily, but can be described by Heidegger´s hermeneutic cir-cle (Heidegger, 2006a, p. 150 e.g.): as having-received-before-hand we take the former use of a concept or an expression and abstract something from this use as having-perceived-before-hand regarding a certain possible representation and connect this abstract characteristic with the new kind of application as having-conceived-beforehand. This process you may call abstraction and the corresponding thinking abstract thinking.

If you apply this to the symbolic use of the concept of the sea, then the having-received-beforehand consists of the primordial usage of the word as the name of the water, which on earth surrounds our continents. From this as having-perceived-beforehand we abstract certain properties of the sea: that all life has its origin in the sea, that the sea can bring death when overflowing the land, that the tides can be seen like coming and going, like birth and death, and that we as embryos have swam in the amniotic liquid, which was similarly salty like the seawater. Thus, we have found characteristics of the sea, which we can associate with birth, life, and death, so that we find a corresponding representation by the sea and so can use the concept of the sea in a new way as an expression for birth, life, and death.

In this abstract resp. symbolic thinking, there is also recognizable some dialectic: the thesis of the factual sea, we can see at the coasts of our continents, meets the antithesis that you can totally ignore this superficial view of the sea, because with the sea is much more connected as what we can see with our pure and poor eyes, and from this we build the synthesis that on the one hand we use the concept of the sea for the actual sea, and on the other hand additionally as a symbol for birth, life, and death. From this perspective you may call thinking dialectical thinking.

This example of dialectical thinking shows clearly that thinking is the imagination of a talk, which also several persons may take part in. By this you can discriminate three different aspects of thinking: the material aspect of the imagined speaking of one or more persons to another or several other persons, who are in some opposite – therefore material – to another (different information, opinions, intentions etc.), the psychic aspect of conceiving the imagined speaking, how this maybe can be differently conceived by different imagined persons motivating to get your own standpoint, and the mindful aspect of understanding what to do and of possible answers to the conceived statement. By this we can *think out* a real drama resp. an entire novel. Normally we think, thinking has only to do something with the mindful level.

But our considerations finally have led to that thinking has material as well as psychic as well as mindful aspects.

You can view human thinking structurally, too, namely that first we look at the whole thing, say the sea, and then analyze this phenomenon and break it down to singular aspects, e.g. the aspect of salty water, the aspect that all life has its origin in the sea etc. like above. Then we again reconstruct the entire fullness of the concept, meaning the sea, and in what manifold ways we can use this concept as a sign and symbolically, and thus add something typically human, what in total this entire phenomenon may represent for us. This way we can call human thinking analytical thinking, too.

The expression dialectical thinking refers more to the general dialogical thinking and thus corresponds more to the being-there mode of the genus, abstract-hermeneutic thinking stresses more the way of thinking as a single person in the being-there mode of the individuum, while analytic thinking by analyzing is rather specifically oriented for use and acting analogue to the being-there mode of the species.

Regarding language you can state the following: by conceiving each way of acting of others and of oneself as an expression or representation of that what one senses as object of the psyche, expectantly feels as object of the mind and plans to do, and/or affectively perceives by one's senses – I want to call this altogether a conceived representation of objective impressions of the person, living being or thing in concern, whereby one meets some being and this being is identified by those impressions – but also by conceiving acts as an expression of something, one has subjectively understood, namely of that, what one as psychic subject affectively discriminating understands about kinds of conditionality, as mindful subject sensationally conceiving understands about possibilities, and as bodily-material subject practically expecting understands about specific difficulties and has a feeling for those difficulties – by this being resp. the existence gets understood and ascertained, and this is nothing substantial, but can be subjectively recognized by deeds resp. exercises at any time in different ways – the ontological difference (Heidegger, 2006a, S.

230)[10] is at least opened, even if not understood first and foremost, for the being-there on the level of the representational self, meaning the difference between being as process of existence and actual met and identified being.

An infant of about four years can distinguish between the appearance of an object and what this object is in fact, e.g. if something looks like a stone but is a sponge. If three years old infants, not yet having reached the level of the representational self, see a sponge knowing it is a sponge, even if it looks like a stone, they will state that it also looks like a sponge and not like a stone (Fonagy, Gergely, Jurist, & Target, 2004, p. 258), the objective appearance resp. the effect of the meeting being, its "utterly meeting and being" reality, is not distinguished from its essence resp. its being, namely that it exists, what shows itself in the subjective process of touching, and this is indeed the ontological difference, the difference between appearance and essence, between some being and being.

The subject-sided understood phenomena resp. what you affectively understood in the verbal communication, sensationally in the hermeneutic circle, and practically in the analysis (see above) – Heidegger calls it "the truth of being" (ibidem), which may shift you into the ecstasy that even something exists rather than nothing – and the object-sided impressions, which however have been subjectively conceived (see above), and by what some being is perceived resp. taken for true ("the truth of the being", ibidem) and identified, determine the expression of being-there, and this expression determines the subject-sided understood of oneself and others, which by communicative exchange can be conceived by the others and oneself, and by this that the being-there is interested in this reaction to one's expression resp. one's own representation for others, one lets oneself determine, i.e. one corrects either one's understanding or one's way of expression or both. But this is only possible, if the being-there meets

---

[10] In "Sein und Zeit" this concept is not mentioned as such, but what it means, namely the difference between to-be as a process and being as a specific living being, which often would be neglected insofar that only the being would be seen and to-be would be not remarked. That something exists is the "truth of being", the "truth of some being" is its identification (ibidem).

other ones, who are so much impressed by the expression of be-ing-there, meaning the representation of one´s being, that the be-ing-there can perceive this change affected by one´s senses as ob-ject of matter, i.e. one determines each other when communi-cating, the other ones are determined by the expression of the being-there, meaning their representation of one´s being, and the being-there by the change because of the making the other ones impressed. Since without language the subjectively understanda-ble conceived cannot be expressed, you may say with Heidegger: Language is "the house of the truth of being" (Heidegger, 2010, p. 10).

Representation implicates the possibility of reproduction, what presupposes a memory. Thus, language is reproduction of contents of memory that is understandable for others, and there is an emotional and a biographic memory (see 2.3). By this our being-there has not yet incorporated the contents of the emo-tional memory – these are only stored contents of our being-there as object of psyche, mind, and matter – until it has further processed these contents as psychic, mindful, or bodily-material subject (see 2.3). Language is conducive to this processing at least by *affects* and *sensations*, because when creating verbal expres-sions, the expressed content of the affective memory is con-ceived, the one of the sensational is sensationally understood, and by this integrated into the biographical one, and only the con-tent of the biographic memory can be directly expressed without any previous processing. This you can recognize by that a human being, who has experienced something quite bad, i.e. a trauma, and wants to tell about it, has difficulties to find the right words, and if asked what happened can answer only slowly and hesi-tantly. But what about processing *feelings* and language?

The problem with feelings and the connected expecta-tions is that necessarily you need new experiences for processing, though this may be not sufficient in all cases. If e.g. you go moun-taineering with a friend and he nearly had fallen into an abyss, you can comfort him that everything is ok and nothing bad has happened, so that his affect of shock and his sensation of anxiety may decrease. But if then you want to go on with him, he proba-bly will refuse, because his feeling of fear and his expectation that something similar might happen again and he would have a bad accident he cannot process in this moment. You cannot discuss actual feelings, but in a safe surrounding speaking about the feelings in a previous situation can actualize corresponding sensations that can be processed and changed into positive sensations strengthening one's psychic-motivational aspect so much that e.g. one exercises by training and broadening one's capabilities and capacities, and thus regulates one's *feelings* by a strengthened self-trust, finally continues performing one's plans and thus integrates everything into one's biographic memory. Thus, here also language helps processing and integrating contents of the emotional memory into the biographical one.

By helping to regulate all emotions, communication makes it possible for the being-there to further process the contents of the emotional memory and to find a verbal expression and thus the right words to class the corresponding content – for feelings after corresponding acts, where speaking also may be such an act – with the biographic memory. Language is neither a reductional representation of the outer world nor does it hint at some inner substance, some solid being or to-be. Since the subject-sided sensationally understood phenomena and the object-sided in the verbal communication subjectively affectively conceived impressions are mindful and psychic and thus related to timeliness and vivid reality, and since the expression is bodily-material and thus spatial, the vivid reality and the timeliness determines resp. conveys the spatiality, and the spatiality connects the vivid reality with the timeliness (however, I already have mentioned above in 2.1 that these three being-there structures are in an absolute dialectical relation).

So, the functions of the human language are on the one hand quite **generally** the regulation of any kind of affects, sensations, and feelings, which may arise by the different impressions as an object of psyche (individual concern), of mind (specific pressure of time or achievement, meaning pressure of expectations), or of matter (general attention or even excitement), so that even traumatic experiences can be processed by the above described way, and on the other hand **in detail** the exchange about intentions to make a mutual arrangement and also to support each other possibly, meaning to found short dated alliances. Finally, and this is the ***specific*** of the human language you will never find in any other form of communication and mutual understanding, language serves for the exchange and appropriation of understood processes about conditionality and possibilities and thus as exchange of temporal and spatial independent representations of reality, so that long-term relationships and friendships can arise, which will exist even then, when it is long ago you have heard from each other.

The specific of this discursivity of language corresponds to the specific of the human being-there, we can talk about our entire being-there including even language itself. This general kind of verbal communication just makes our individual reflexivity possible. The meaning and all new creations of words develop from hermeneutic circles, and all in all in a certain way, this is an image of the human community: words resp. meanings die out, new ones are born, and there are familial relations quite like that among men.

The verbal expression reproduces reality, and by this it may be reductional, but it can also express more than what is prevailing. We can verbally express what is just impressing and moving us (as an object), what has impressed or moved us, or what might move or impress us in the future, verbally we can go forward into the future ("if I do this, then this will come, and then I can do this, and that will come then etc."), to plan and to draft our future life, or we can go backward into the past ("this has happened, because I made this, what I did because this has happened, because I made that etc.") to pin down our past life and the experiences made then, to resume this and make our experiences usable for our further life by corresponding conclusions, and we can arrive in the present and act ("to reach this, I must do that, and therefore this, and therefore again that, and that I can do now, because these conditions are fulfilled already, so that I know what to do") better and better oriented where we just have arrived.

Since the verbal expression reproduces reality, it gives us information about this, i.e. the verbal expression is a very special part of the ecstasy of information (see 2.1). Besides, it becomes generally clear that the ecstasy of information does not work without communication, i.e. the ecstasy of information *is* basically nothing else but communication. Thus, it is shown that the communication about origin, future and arrival plays the decisive role, whether the being-there is on the way to perfect love or on the way into a neurotic, psychotic resp. traumatic or psychotic-depressive resp. addiction-like disturbance. If you want, you may call this a philosophical foundation of the **importance of the dialogue in psychotherapy**. Processing, development, or healing always begin in the mode of genus and are conveyed by communication, must then be continued and accepted by the being-there in the mode of individuum to be implemented in the mode of species by corresponding acts or interactions. If the goal is still not reached, the circulation must begin from the start in the mode of genus to conceive and understand what went wrong and/or is missing. If the process gets interrupted in one of the three modes, it comes to no healing, no development resp. to no processing.

Further statements about thinking, reason, and language as well as their development you will find in the 4th chapter of "Nature and Love" (Kolb, 2017e, p. 57 et seqq.). There, the linguistic theories of Austin and Searle are viewed and modified by being-there analysis.

3.4. The Ability to Love on the Level of the Sexual Self

In preparation for the topic of this chapter I want to yield to the first five developmental levels of the self once more, to depict how children develop in dealing with other people and which forms and patterns of relationships evolve by this. On the level of the physical self, children see in their mother a mirror only, which provides them certain common insights concerning activity and passivity. On the level of the social self, their mother is already more of a counterpart, whom on the one hand they prompt something, but whom on the other hand they must and will regard. On the level of the teleological self, children perceive that they need their mother for protection, and that they themselves must be cautious not to lose her. On the level of the intentional self, children perceive that they can and need not reach everything alone, but that they can agree to short dated alliances with their mother, too, where everybody, both children and their mothers, have prospects of certain advantages resp. of accomplishing certain intentions.

On the level of the representational self, children finally learn how useful it is to bond with others and have long term relationships and friendships instead of short dated alliances like on the previous level of the intentional self. Because to be able to deal better and better with one's own deficiencies, it is advisable, on the one hand again and again to exchange views about this as steadily as possible, in order that one conceives and understands oneself better and better and learns to make oneself conceivable and understandable for others better and better, too. Since, however, this implies some corresponding trust in the other one in concern, in order that this one does not use his knowledge about me against myself, it is recommendable on the other hand, to agree with long term friendships with other ones, where I can be rather secure that they meet me with benevolence, i.e. they are interested resp. want that I feel good and are concerned if not. Therefore, such good friends again and again will draw my attention to my strong points as well as to my deficiencies by their honest feedback of their concern, so that I can better and better deal with them and shall be guilty less and less, meaning that I act more and more responsible-reflected and human. Vice versa I shall help them to get such a self-awareness as well.

A temporally and spatially independent interest for the other one that he feels good, a goodwill towards the friend, which is not dependent from something useful or does not base on something pleasant, but gives as such something to the human being-there and fosters the development of someone's virtuousness (resp. capability to love in my terminology), corresponds to the perfect friendship according to Aristoteles (Aristoteles, 1985, p. 184 et seqq., 1156a and b). The importance of perfect friendship for our capability to love resp. for that we come closer and closer to perfect love is shown by the following: if I am seized by something or someone and then expect to reach something, if thus I want to have something in the broadest sense, again and again, there may be circumstances, which let me fail, so that I have deluded myself and am disappointed. Then and only then, when seen from my mind, I merely expected to be absolutely seized by my seizedness of somebody, this is to-be instead of to-have, and if I really was seized like that seen from my psyche, if thus being seized (without wanting to have) of somebody was sufficient for me as such and fulfilled me perfectly, then I never could delude myself or be disappointed resp. indignant. My sensational understanding, connected with my expectations, of my seizedness, which then would be my entire for-the-sake-of-which, would be true, because there could be no delusion, since I would indeed be absolutely seized by my seizedness, and immediate, because my understanding would immediately relate to my absolute seizedness and would be mediated by nothing else, i.e. I would love myself perfectly (true and immediate understanding of my entire for-the-sake-of-which, s. 2.1) and would have reached perfect love, since perfect self-love and perfect love of others are absolutely mutually dependent; in my absolute seizedness of the other I indeed would love him perfectly, too.

If seen from the psyche I was absolutely fulfilled, I could, seen from the mind, have no other expectation but to be absolutely seized by my seizedness, i.e. mind and psyche would be absolutely united and both with the bodily-material aspect, too, since there would be no delusion and thus no kinds of oppositeness. If vice versa seen from the mind, I solely had the expectation to be absolutely seized by my seizedness, this could only be the case, if I would be absolutely seized by my seizedness in fact, so that here as well, there could be no tension between mind and psyche and thus also not to the bodily-material aspect. If the human being-there, namely we ourselves, could succeed to be absolutely seized by the seizedness of one single other being-there, then one could have no other expectation concerning the other one but to be absolutely fulfilled by this seizedness, and by this one would love the other perfectly, i.e. perfect love would be reached. Thus, the absolute seizedness of one other human being would be sufficient to acquire perfect love.

Let us now come to the development of the sexual self: on the developmental level of the representational self, after children for the first time have conceived the danger that they could lose the affiliation to their community, to their family, because of their deficiencies, they seek to make themselves useful and develop specific strategies (plans for acting) for this, which they perform in a specific mood, general stands of values and individual attitudes (a stand is the general bodily-material aspect of a disposition, an attitude is the individual psychic-motivational one, and a mood the specific mindful one (Kolb, 2017c)). This altogether relates to certain representations resp. a certain Weltanschauung to deal better with certain situations, to conceive them better, to plan and to act better. Dispositions you can methodically analyze and characterize by means of the five contrarieties active-passive, subjective-objective, discontinuous-continuous, linear-circular, and temporal-spatial, or you can classify them by these contrarieties as perceptional patterns and thus fix them materially. Since all contrarieties can be characterized by these five basic kinds of diversity (Kolb, 2017a), such an analysis is complete.

Regarding the opposite active-passive you can orient yourself resp. your mood (influencing your strategies), your stands of values and your attitudes either to that it is better to actively approach other people to become acquainted with them by their reactions i.e. to certain kinds of provocation, or contrarily that it is better to stay passive and wait how the one in concern will act by her- or himself to assess them this way. Concerning the opposite subjective-objective you can orient yourself to that it is better to assert yourself, to prevail, and as subject to exercise power over other ones, or contrarily to comply instead, to serve, and to be there for the objective concerns of others. Based on the opposite discontinuous-continuous you can either take up the position that it is better to indeed erratically test all possibilities, to get stimulations as much as possible, in order that it does something for you and does not become boring, or contrarily to be concerned about safety, and e.g. to continuously cleave to relationships, even if you must relinquish many things. In relation to the opposite linear-circular you directly approach your goal and to be zealous for linear progress, or contrarily you accept setbacks and patiently wait for opportunities, till the other ones are pleased and only then you may regulate your objectives.

Related to the opposite temporal-spatial you make inquiries either where problems come from and by what tasks are set to you, which future ideals are worthwhile, and which momentary solving steps must be performed, i.e. you freely move in the three ecstasies of origin, future, and arrival (Kolb, 2017a), to improve your technique of acting more and more without considerations of the space of other ones, so you stress timeliness, or by contrast you embark, so to say share space with other ones (thus stressing spatiality), extensively exchange with others how you represent reality, and if somebody hurts or even damages you, then you change your negative sensations about that into a planning resp. reactive understanding, certainly the other one did not do that intentionally, perhaps you have invited her or him, e.g. to exploit you, or the other one has some illness or handicap, which is why you should help him or her, i.e. you interpret the behavior of the other one, so that you can forgive her or him or that he or she even seems to be innocent and you are sorry, reacting correspondingly by changing your own acting (no more invitation to exploit), or by contrast helping the other one with her or his illness or disability.

If you take together each of the first alternatives of the five opposites, you will get a life strategy centered on your own self and assuming it is necessary first to consolidate yourself before you support others, while the other alternatives altogether emphasize the necessity of self-surrender before you care for yourself. Both can be related to the two main categories of problems a community must solve, namely regulating outer contacts (protecting against danger and providing resources) and achieving harmony as much as possible within the community, in order that everybody can feel as well as possible.

The one, who wants to escape from becoming outcast, should make oneself useful at least in one of these both categories, where the life strategy centered on your own self and assuming it is necessary first to consolidate yourself before you support others best fits the regulation of outer contacts. Therefore, the one in concern will present one´s abilities and capabilities as positive as possible, i.e. one will try to attract attention and will express that one can achieve and work pretty much. To contribute to reaching harmony as much as possible, optimally fits the necessity of self-surrender, and the person in concern therefore will decidedly try for harmony and correspondingly appear as helpful resp. will express this in one´s acting.

Typically, at least for our culture, boys acquire the first attitude in puberty and girls the second one. Fitting this, empirical findings prove that the contact with an attractive woman stimulates heterosexual men to strike and to show what they can. Correspondingly, heterosexual women are on their helpful behavior, if they have or just have had contact with a man attractive for them. This may have several causes, corresponding role models, messages by media, to mention only a few environmental influences. However, choosing your attitude and manner, how and in which realms of your community you want to make yourself useful, will be later influenced by, how your sexuality develops, whereby I mean all stirrings and impulses that show up, when the sexual development elicits more and more emotions and new intentions.

Since women as mothers surrender themselves to their infant because of nursing and men as fathers of a new-born baby are protecting both mother and child and providing all necessary things for both meaning to regulate the outside contacts of this community of three, I call the dispositional orientation towards the necessity of self-surrender before you care for yourself female principle and the corresponding orientation towards the necessity of self-consolidation before you support others male principle.

I have called each of this principle and not disposition, because you can match different stands, attitudes, and moods with the female and male principle each. Male and female principle are basic relational patterns of perceiving, judging, and expecting, and this indicates the inter-existentiality of these concepts. The older children of a classical nuclear family grow, the more important it gets for parents or man and woman, at least in our culture, to distribute the different tasks for the family anew, so that not only the husband is regulating the outside contacts and the wife does not alone care for harmony in the family. Women e.g. can go working, when their children are at school, and men can keep the household as well cooking for the family to make everybody feel as comfortable as possible.

If male and female principle are not connected in the being-there, if you do not overcome this oppositeness, but live out one of the both extremely, if one of these principles exclusively leads the relation between being-there and being-in-the-world, then earlier or later this must come to a delusion resp. to a disappointment (sensation), because one-sidedly geared to, each principle requires much power and energy, which is not accessible any more by greater encumbrances or at the latest when you grow old. Further, it is important for the development of children that their parents are good with this oppositeness and thus create a sustainable stability, where their children can raise up. One parent usually is overwhelmed to give this stability.

If you fail with the extremely lived out female principle, then you as psychic subject consider the situation you have perceived as object of matter, if from your perspective you only note the aspect that it is necessary to surrender yourself and, however, you cannot ease the problems and needs of the other ones, if so you finally realize that your life strategy has failed, you do not consider this as a situation of your own deficiencies or those of the world as you would do on the level of the representational self, but as a situation of *missing appreciation* – partly you find yourself not worthy enough to be loved, because you cannot or can no more make yourself useful for others, partly the world is not enough appreciating you, is not grateful for your own efforts and renouncements (you have given more than you got), so that you can no more get enthusiastic about your being-in-the-world and can no more develop compassion or zeal (feeling) for anything and finally only feel sorrow for everything, even especially at yourself. Here, the connection with the sixth sense of the suspecting foresight becomes obvious, how I have described it in "Dasein, um zu lieben" (Kolb, 2017a). On the level of affects the ones of discrepancy prevail, a shift of or mixture with the basic negative affects of being-there.

But if you fail with the male principle, meaning that from your perspective you only note the aspect of the necessity of self-consolidation and cannot consolidate your position, if you finally realize that your life strategy has failed, you also judge the perceived situation not as a situation of your own deficiencies, but as a situation of missing appreciation as well – partly you find yourself not worthy enough to be loved, because you even cannot care for yourself, partly the world is not enough appreciating you, pays no adequate attention for your efforts and successes and gives or has given you not enough opportunities to develop and unfold your potential, so that you can no more get enthusiastic about your being-in-the-world and develop compassion or zeal (feeling) for anything, but finally only care for yourself jealously. Here, the connection with the sixth sense of the suspecting foresight becomes obvious, too (see above). On the level of affects the ones of discrepancy prevail as well.

When each partner of a relationship also views the common situation from the other perspective of these both ones and thus notes the corresponding alternative aspect, both can realize the advantage and disadvantage of their own life strategy and by this overcome the oppositeness of both aspects, gather more and more experiences. They become wiser to the effect that they conceive more and more, when which one of both life strategies is the better one, if they understand each other more and more immediately and truly in the for-the-sake-of-which, meaning if they love each other more and more perfectly. Then both have found something of their sexual self, as I want to call it, because only by realizing the other aspect, their own self-choice of the corresponding gender role becomes clear to them, whereby women also might have chosen the typical male role and men the typical female role. Now, they can constructively use their feelings of missing appreciation to face up to their cohesiveness with their partner, and the more this togetherness develops, the more this elicits inspiration and compassion, and the more, this drives back the respective sorrow or jealousy by exercising and testing the alternatives again and again, so that during their development on the level of the sexual self they mutually find themselves more and more, and by this their love to each other and to themselves can develop better and better.

If then the opposite self-care and care for others was totally overcome, perfect love would be reached, and you would have perfectly found the other one and yourself. The more often and consistently we are inspired in every-day life, the more we gratefully can appreciate our origin, future, and arrival in every-day life, the further we have come on our way to perfect love. Because of the grateful appreciation namely, we strive after more and more true information about origin, future, and arrival of resp. in our momentary situation, a necessary and sufficient condition to more and more near the utopia of perfect love (see 2.2).

My past description naturally concerns the ideal case of the human development towards perfect love only. Disturbances you can realize on the different developmental levels by the following: on the level of the *physical* self, if there is a disturbance and being-there one does not find oneself any further or even has lost oneself, as object of matter one does not affectively by senses perceive in some realms, what one brings about or elicits in one´s physical environment by one´s behavior, as psychic subject one cannot conceive one´s position and therefore as object of psyche be sensible of nothing the right way, and one also does not know how to understand as mindful subject what measures to adopt; correspondingly on the level of the *social* self, as object of matter one does not affectively by senses perceive in some realms, how much one e.g. annoys, disturbs, molests, hinders, endangers, or even damages other ones, as psychic subject one conceives what happens, as if only one oneself gets impaired, and therefore one is angry as object of psyche or as object of mind full of rage and tries to take vengeance, since one understands oneself unfairly disadvantaged because of bad life conditions, which as psychic subject one believes to realize resp. one wrongly conceives that way – one is at odds with one´s *origin* so to say; on the level of the *teleological* self, as object of matter one does not affectively by senses perceive in some realms, and also does not conceive as psychic subject, how little well-planned one has organized one´s life, one judges all that happens, as if there was chaos all around and correspondingly senses great angst, and as mindful subject looks for possibilities, how one can protect or help oneself best – one is anxious about the *future*; on the level of the *intentional* self, as object of matter one does not affectively by senses perceive in some realms, and also does not conceive as psychic subject, how little tolerating one is with oneself or others, how little one can wait, and how little one tries for confederations, one judges what happens, as if there were only throwbacks and one is left alone, as if everything was hopeless and nobody could help, so that as object of psyche most of all one senses suffering for that, and as mindful subject looks for possibilities mostly in vain, how one can stand one's despair – one has the feeling to be arrived in a world full of suffering (painful *arrival*); on the level of the *representational* self, as object of matter one does not affectively by senses perceive in some realms, and also does not conceive as psychic subject that other people represent reality differently for themselves, judge things and happenings according to other viewpoints, and how little trust one has in others or in oneself, since one's lack of understanding leads to misconceptions again and again. As psychic subject one judges what happens, as if either oneself or other ones are guilty, meaning one condemns oneself and/or others, so that one as object of psyche or mind mainly senses or feels disappointment, indignation, shame, and guilt therefore, and as bodily-material or mindful subject one too little looks for friendship with others and mostly in vain for possibilities, how one can overcome one's own deficiencies or that of the world – one has got the feeling to exist in a world, which gives *information* about to many things filling one with indignation.

On the level of the *sexual* self, as object of matter one does not affectively by senses perceive in some realms, and does not conceive as psychic subject as well that one's own attitude that only self-surrender or else only self-consolidation be necessary, is not adequate and by time leads to a chronic fatigue depression or to egocentrism and isolation, because one's lopsided life strategy will always fail earlier or later, in old age at the latest, when the power lacks for that. Therefore, as psychic subject one views one's failure, as if oneself or the world was worthless, so that one as object of psyche senses a deep disappointment as a result of more and more strongly negative affects that here something is wrong. As mindful subject one mostly in vain looks for possibilities how to overcome one´s worthlessness or the lacking appreciation of the world – one has the feeling to live in a world, in which there is no appreciation or no love, because of which one cannot get excited and develop compassion for anything. Usually this catastrophe eventuates, when the being-there has come together with an intimate partner, who either pursues the same life strategy or who can develop the sensational-expecting understanding neither of oneself nor of others in their or one´s own for-the-sake-of-which, because this partner already does not progress or even regresses on one of the previous developmental levels.

Again and again, and more and more to realize, what I effect, again and again constructively to use and more and more by this to overcome the anger/the disgust by hardship situations and the rage/the abhorrence about concrete iniquities coming from the past, the anxiety about the future, cause I have taken responsibility for that, and especially because of my mortality, or the fear of something concrete, e.g. of a certain way to die, the suffering by hopelessness or the mourning about the momentary situation and shame because of my being-there and feelings of guilt because of something concrete and the disappointment about the world or indignation because of something concrete, and to get enthusiastic about everyday-life with or without an intimate partner again and again by appreciating my origin, future, and arrival more and more, by being grateful for it – as long as I succeed in that, and this must be "The Claim of Reason" (Cavell, 1979), I am on the way, which is the goal. The way to perfect love, the steady advancement of my ability to love – I am not only required by my being-there, I can also fulfill this claim encompassing my whole life de facto again and again.

Our being-there always remains connected with our mother because of our origin. This connection is so to say anchored in our mode of genus inextricably, since to be human is recursively defined as to have a human mother. From this connection then arise all possible forms of being together of being-there (in the mode of genus) with other people. These are the forms of unity as extension, e.g. if somebody is in a coma and we care for her or him, as our being-there had had it with our mother at the beginning of our existence, the forms of controversy and tolerance, as our being-there had exercised with our mother on the level of the social self, forms of mutual protecting, as our being-there had rehearsed with our mother on the level of the teleological self, forms of mutual help and support, and collaboration and short-term confederations, as our being-there had learnt with our mother on the level of the intentional self, forms of verbal communication, of exchange, and of longer-term friendship, of counselling and discussion within a language community or nation or the whole humanity, as our being-there had gained with our mother on the level of the representational self, and forms of sexual relationships, whereby our being-there on the level of the sexual self tries to restore the primordial unity, as this has existed with our mother, with the partner, and thus strives for the utopian goal of perfect love.

These forms of relationship can proceed both constructively and destructively. In the destructive case the form of unity as extension becomes negligence, the form of controversy quarrel and war, the form of mutual protection forsaking, the form of collaboration deception, the form of friendship exploitation and violation of human dignity, and the form of sexual intimate relationship fornication and sexual misuse.

How can you now describe the approach to sexuality from being-there analytic perspective? According to the female principle one´s main concern is the harmony within the community that everybody feels as content and well as possible, and for this one readily postpones one´s own interests and necessities. She observes and analyzes, which desires and cravings the other ones have, and seeks to satisfy them, as the case may be. Thereby she questions, which cravings and desires could disturb the harmony of the community in concern (e.g. also of her momentary intimate partnership), if they were either satisfied or not, so that by corresponding actions she can strengthen her power and influence. By this problematization of desiring, under which circumstances its fulfilling or its not-fulfilling can disturb or foster the harmony, we have hit an essential characteristic of the female sexuality, how I want to call the sexual practice homing in on the female principle.

Correspondingly, I want to name the male sexuality as that sexual practice homing in on the male principle, the essential characteristic of which is that when you desire there is only one problem, namely if and how you can get satisfaction and how much you can increase your power by this, or how much it is weakened possibly. If a man then feels consolidated, he can e.g. strengthen the resources of his community by own descendants and thus increase his influence within his community, even if he weakens his force by the associated sexual act. In the end, concerning both forms of sexuality, you strive to strengthen your own power in your currently own form of female resp. male performance (Kolb, 2017c, p. 148 et seqq., 4th and 5th chapter). At least in the beginning of sexuality, it seems to be about power and not about love. Using the example of the antique Greeks, I have shown (ibidem), how by the male sexuality the striving after power has changed at least concerning Plato and Aristotle, and more and more has geared to perfect love by pursuing truth or blessedness (eudaimonia).

3.5. Psychoanalytic Concepts Viewed from Being-There Analysis

Let us now come to the relationship between the ability to love, superego formation, and ability to sublimate, and considerations about, what is meant by consciousness, unconscious, and dreaming:

If one has internalized ethical virtues (general behavioral rules of a specific community), e.g. those according to Aristotle (Aristoteles, 1985), in terms of the psychoanalytic theory you would say, one has developed a superego formation. As long as this is rudimentary, being-there one obeys these virtues, only because she or he fears negative consequences like some punishment. But the more infants understand their parents in the for-the-sake-of-which, the more they love their parents perfectly, the more willingly they will assume their parents' ethical virtues, and if they act accordingly, the perception of the virtuous consequences of their acts relate to joy and pleasure. The more the rules and norms of the superego formation are understood via understanding their parents′ for-the-sake-of-which, the more developed it is in terms of the psychoanalytic theory. But if something confronts this joy and pleasure, e.g. an enormous fear of the austerity of their parents or the apprehension, one parent could be beleaguered and break down, if the children do not bestir themselves and act well, if so to say the pleasure serves as compensation, then the understanding of the for-the-sake-of-which of their parents is limited, and the superego formation cannot develop any further. So, as long as joy and pleasure relate to love resp. growing true and immediate understanding, the ethical virtues get cultivated more and more resp. the superego formation of children matures more and more.

If somebody has joy and pleasure relating to the five dianoetic virtues reason, science, craftsmanship, prudence, and wisdom (Aristoteles, 1985), this is expressed in terms of psychoanalysis by that the person in concern can sublime. She or he then has pleasure gain independent of sexuality. Since the dianoetic virtues form the ethical ones, here a coherence becomes distinct between sublimation and the development of the superego formation, which as far as I know is not mentioned in the psychoanalytic literature: the bigger the capability to love, the bigger is one′s capability to sublime, and both influences the superego formation, so that it gets more and more mature.

As I explained in "Liebe, Macht und Sexualität" (Kolb, 2017c) in the 9th chapter, *consciousness* is a state where you continuously can compare contents of your memory with other memory contents, with imaginations, and with happenings we perceive, have perceived (and memorize), and imagine or have imagined. By contrast to this, I additionally have introduced the concept of *awareness*, which exclusively occurs by us humans, when comparing (1) in the mode of genus, how we subjectively conceive, have conceived, or can conceive, (2) in the mode of species, how we implement, have implemented, or can implement our decisions by acting as skillful as possible, and (3) in the mode of individuum, if I realize, where comparing my representations with each other by the corresponding seizedness and judging leads me to, has led me to, or can lead me to decisions resp. to which imaginations of the possibilities of being, between which I can choose then. By awareness I use the functions of the circle of the wise or responsible acting (ibidem). Concerning the contents of memory when being able to compare like that, it is about the ones of the emotional memory and their integration into the biographic one, which is only possible with awareness.

Insofar everything is unconscious, what is not conscious to us, what we cannot compare with something else, either because we have got no factual access to compare data, or because we renounce or have renounced ourselves for any reason whatsoever. In the last case the comparison is opened up to us in terms of Heidegger, i.e. principally accessible, but we have renounced it, we prefer to keep ourselves uncertain, since we do not integrate certain emotional contents in our biographic memory, because we could get to excited about it, and by this we hinder ourselves to be able to compare, unless the memory content is elicited by something else. The counterpart of consciousness resp. being able to compare is a disability, but the counterpart of awareness is keeping oneself in uncertainty or in the lack of clarity. Because of renouncing yourself you are not conscious of certain stirrings or impulses of your own, you cannot compare, because it is not integrated in the biographic memory and in the actual moment not elicited by something else. This realm of that, what is not conscious for us resp. we are not aware of, is the actual phenomenon of the *psychoanalytic unconsciousness as opposite to awareness*, an excellent phenomenon, namely "such one, what for one thing and most commonly is *not* showing itself, what is *concealed* in contrast to that, what is showing first and foremost [in this case the so called unconscious stirrings or impulses or Freudian slips], but at the same time is something that belongs to that showing first and foremost, in fact that way that it represents its sense and reason" (Heidegger, 2006a, p. 35, own translation). Unawareness is always vague, is suppression, awareness is clarifying and removes suppression.

But what can be a reason resp. what does it mean ontologically that we in our being-there have chosen uncertainty, that we have renounced our awareness? In the mode of genus, if we do not want to compare something we have conceived and thus renounce our being-there by keeping ourselves in uncertainty, the perceived opposites are too big, the corresponding affects too strong, so that we do not have enough *strength* to face up to it, and therefore separate these affects. In the mode of species, the practical difficulties seem too big for our being-there, and the corresponding feelings too bad, so that we do not presume enough abilities and capabilities to manage these difficulties resp. have not enough *courage* to face up to it, and therefore cope with resp. get over our feelings either by apathy or by actionism. In the mode of individuum, what we being-there conceive or have conceived as perceived contrarieties, and the corresponding sensations are too encumbering, so that we do not have enough *self-confidence* to come to good decisions considering the severe possibilities that may come to us, and to plan correspondingly, and therefore defend our sensations. The relation of being-there and world, meaning the relationship between being-there and our being-in-the-world, our life, is disturbed.

The most common manner, how we begin to keep ourselves in uncertainty and thus create unawareness, is that we do not take an interest in the effect of our acting on others. Either we separate the affective perception already in this moment, because we lack the strength to deal with the effects resp. with reality, or we admittedly process the fact that we have erred or are upset, but then defend all resulting sensations, each form of self-concern, because we lack the self-confidence to decide well and avoid catastrophes, or if we conceive after all, we fall into apathy or actionism, because we lack the courage to perform our decisions and act effectively problem solving.

As individual we are conscious, if we are seized by something, by a representation from our memory or by something we have (affectively) perceived and then have made a concept resp. a representation of it, and then compare this representation with other representations with a corresponding seizedness. At that it can be about a waking consciousness, if our being-there is in contact with our true world, or about the consciousness during a dream or a daydream resp. a trance, if we are in contact with another "world" (former times, phantasy etc.). The difference between these two kinds of consciousness may not always be clear for us. As trance I denote every state, in which we do not sleep, but are disconnected from the actual happenings, i.e. not conscious in the mode of genus, whereby this state lasts a perceptible moment, and we say afterwards e.g., we had thought about something a little bit longer, remembered something or imagined or considered.

If awareness occurs when dreaming, these dreams are often denoted as lucid dreams. As in total, you can see both in the mode of genus and in the mode of species and of individuum that I can get swept up by the typical human awareness as distinct from the simple consciousness, which also animals can have, in the three temporal ecstasies of origin (awareness as genus), of future (awareness as individual), and of arrival (awareness as species), but also in the spatial ecstasy of information, if e.g. I regain certain forgotten or suppressed contents of my memory (Kolb, 2017c).

You may ask now, which evolutionary progress dreaming has given. What should it be good for that we are dreaming at night when sleeping instead of simply sleeping like a log? Neurobiologists have found out that when sleeping activities spring from the brainstem (e.g. when the temperature of the body descends too much), which seemingly chaotically lead to activities in the whole thalamocortical system, which we get a dream-consciousness by, which by the limbic system, which is activated by this as well, gets a certain seizedness of the different stimuli, so that we can compare the activated and emotionally incensed contents – this is the dream-consciousness as a state of being able to compare. To give these different stimuli as a self-organizing system a sense, so means Thomas Metzinger, the brain tells itself a somehow fitting fairy tale (Metzinger, 2014, S. 211). The only assured adaptational advantage, which mammals would have by dreaming resp. by activating the brainstem, would be from biologically view that also during sleep the body temperature would be regulated (ibidem). That there is at least one more adaptational advantage, the following empirical findings may show:

1. When during an experiment one hindered experimental subjects to dream, but not to sleep by consequently waking them up, if they had a REM-phase of sleeping, after three or four nights they got hallucinations and delusions, so that one had to stop the experiment.

2. If you compare the brain-structure of animals without REM-sleep like e.g. the ant-eater with the one of humans, you will see that proportionally we would need such a big volume of frontal and temporal lobe that we hardly could kick it down the road in a wheelbarrow.

Since in the frontal and temporal lobe the so-called reminiscences of the day are stored, i.e. all possible information we indeed have recorded, but not progressed, these finding fits with Freud's assertion that such reminiscences elicit dreams, so that these are progressed, and the memory space is released again. The adaptational advantage thus entails saving "hardware" (frontal and temporal lobe) and therefore developing a "software" (the possibility to dream). If you cannot store anything in the frontal and temporal lobe, because there is no more space, you are going to get hallucinations and delusions.

Researching this "software" we get the possibility to discover certain unconscious variants of the information processing of our brain, which during the waking consciousness proceed mostly covertly, meaning not consciously, and can be realized during daydream at the most. Freud called this research the royal road to the unconscious. What Freud called the unconscious and I "certain unconscious variants of the information processing", which do not attract our attention in the waking consciousness, these variants do not use the comparison between some representations we have made of our environment, of others and of ourselves, but only use our contingency-detection mechanism, which already little infants have from birth (Fonagy, Gergely, Jurist, & Target, 2004, p. 208). From the beginning our brain indeed has the tendency to condense different simultaneous stimuli to an overall impression (Metzinger denotes this as "telling fairy tales" when dreaming), wherein I have seen the basis of the contingency-detection mechanism (Kolb, 2017c, p. 36 et seqq., 2nd chapter).

Thus, each kind of progressing (of information being received by us as stimuli of our senses) is unconscious, which does not use the comparison with representations out of our memory. Therefore Freud's method of free association, where you use nothing else but this contingency-detection mechanism, is so successful in the research of our dreams. You may call the corresponding level of information processing sub-personal, too, instead of unconscious, if you assume that a person is characterized by a shell of representations figuratively speaking, which it sounds through (from Latin personare), so that sub-personal means that this shell of representations is not used and therefore no person can sound through.

A further phenomenon you can explain by unconscious or sub-personal information processing is the so-called nanny-sleep. A nanny, by creating a firm association between any utterance of noises of the infant she must look after and her own impetus to wake up, can on the one hand be fast asleep, on the other hand get real immediately, as soon as the infant in concern awakes and gets restless. It is possible that our entire wake-sleep-rhythm and maybe still other rhythms, e.g. our rhythm of breathing, gets partly regulated by certain associations and thus to a high percentage sub-personally. Insofar the conscious observing of our breathing can give us similar information like Freud's analysis of dreams.

Especially if aware as individual, when understanding and consciously confronted with the choice between the different possibilities of my capability-to-be, but also if aware as species, when after a decision I must consider an execution by action as skillful as possible, and if aware as genus, when conceiving and getting conscious of my own representations of the world, of others, and of myself, which I underlay my perceptions, so that I must bear the burden of my seizedness – as soon as I realize in each case that I am a subject, namely a mindful, a material, and a psychic one, I am totally on my own, I get the imagination of loneliness and experience this loneliness, which is connected with corresponding emotions of pain, suffering, and grief, but also of flare, anger, and rage because of having been thrown into this situation of loneliness, and of shock, anxiety, and fear never to get out of this loneliness. This loneliness so-to-say overshadows the whole relationship to my being-in-the-world, all my life. In this loneliness as subject therefore I am totally thrown back onto my own self and thus consciously go through the suffering of being separated from perfect love. As subject I am subject to my loneliness and prompted to stir and to do something. Therefore, awareness can be denoted as some typically human being active, which can promote me on my way to perfect love, so that Meister Eckart meant, suffering would be the fastest steed to God, and awareness constitutes the goal of each psychoanalytically reasoned treatment, meaning that both practitioners and treated ones get thrown back onto their own self. By this for both, the development of their capability to love is fostered, what by Freud, however, has not been formulated this way.

When considering one's self, the following appears: On the one hand, there is the phenomenon of the I or ego, something conscious resp. personal, what everybody can distinguish by comparison with other ones and things (conscious perception) as that, what usually gives a shout, directly and often loudly, and sounds through the shell of one's representations of the world, of others, and of oneself. Partly the I resp. ego belongs to the self, partly being-there one deludes oneself, when mistaking certain ego-parts for a part of one's self. The ego has (1) a psychic aspect, in how far one being-there means to conceive oneself and to know the score about oneself, what one expresses e.g. by narratives about oneself and one's previous development, (2) a mindful aspect, for what possibilities of the capability-to-be one being-there believes to be able to decide, which roles and functions are available to one being-there, and (3) a material aspect, in how far one being-there spatially and temporally can distinguish one's own body from everything else. The ego is relative and depending on the actual situation.

On the other hand, there is the phenomenon of the self, which in all its affluence is a distinguished phenomenon in terms of Heidegger (see below), in great part an unconscious resp. sub-personal part, which we only approximately and very hard can recognize, preferably by the research of dreams or by the conscious experiencing of states of trance, so that the thus recognized parts of the self are added to the ego. The self is absolute and independent of situations, place and time. In the utopia of perfect love ego resp. I and the self would be the same. Phenomenon in a distinguished sense means according to Heidegger that here something (the self) reports very indirectly, namely "such one, what for one thing and most commonly is *not* showing itself, what is *concealed* in contrast to that, what is showing first and foremost [in this case the ego resp. the I], but at the same time is something that belongs to that showing first and foremost, in fact that way that it represents its sense and reason" (Heidegger, Sein und Zeit, 2006a, p. 35, own translation).

The existence of the phenomenon of the self, which extends the phenomenon of the ego, stands and falls with, whether the human being-there has a sense and reason (not a cause) or not. The phenomenon of the self needs no cause and cannot have any, since it is absolute and not from this (relative) world. Formerly I have shown that sense and reason of our being-there is the development of our capability to love in the direction of perfect love (Kolb, 2017a). This makes sense, because it is witnessed by our being-there, and this development is a practical possibility (see 2.2), so that this development of our capability to love, even if we do not reach the utopia of perfect love, represents not only the sense, but is also reasonable for our being-there. Seen from our self, concerning the narratives about ourselves and our own development, only the consideration of the previous development of our capability to love is important, what then can motivate us positively. Only those ego-functions have a meaning, which more and more enable us to act so that we ideally do not delude ourselves, and regarding the bodily-material aspect it more and more is about to give and take alike much space and time for others and for ourselves, so that all contrarieties can be more and more overcome. Thus, because our being-there has sense and reason, the existence of our self is demonstrated (a proof is neither possible nor reasonable). If our being-there would be without sense and reason, we would be machines, as e.g. Metzinger means (Metzinger, 2014), machines, which only persuade themselves resp. subjectively take for granted that they have a self, but which otherwise would be totally technically constructible. If we actually would be machines, we really would have no self, but if not, then there is a sense and a reason, and thus a self.

3.6. Levels of Experience and Language

If we humans are or become conscious of a situation (for definition and explanation see footnote p. 29, chapter 2.2), we are on the one hand consciously confronted with the world and all we meet there, but on the other hand also with our self-process, which steadily is changing in the encounter with everything of the world. An important part of this process is our bodiliness, i.e. all our stirrings and impulses, which convey us i. a. our liveliness. However, if we are in the so called "as-if-mode" of experiencing[11], namely related to fantasized possibilities by putting ourselves in an imagined situation, e.g. of others, and if we then perceive ourselves from the perspective of somebody else in our real and current situation, we are reflexive resp. reflected and say about us from the corresponding level of language that we <u>have</u> a body (but meaning a corpus). Otherwise, if we are seized by our impulses, we <u>are</u> our body and are in the so called "equivalence-mode", and, since immediately influenced by our own current stirrings and impulses, we are prereflexive. The difference between corpus and body is that our corpus only means the self-processes, which are knowable by natural or medical sciences and are objective in this sense, meaning our physical processes of growth and decay resp. the entirety of our interwoven physical processes, which can be comprehended by others, while the body means all our self-processes, from which we directly resp. immediately and insofar subjectively sense something by our stirrings and impulses. These processes principally cannot be witnessed by

---

[11] Experiencing is the way, how, in a situation, we affectively perceive, sensationally judge, and, by expectantly feeling out, imagine sections of our being-in-the-world. It is the experiencing, what we meet or encounter in the world, which makes our impulses change.

scientific methods. The duality of corpus and body is like that one in quantum physics, where everything has the characteristic of a corpuscle and of a wave. Besides the as-if-mode and the equivalence-mode of experiencing there still is the reality-mode, if we experience our own effects of our being-in-the-world, namely that, what the world mirrors us back. These three modes are in an absolute dialectical relationship, as you may easily show, i.e. two of them convey the third, and this one between both others.

From our stirrings and impulses and thus from our bodiliness the different fundamental phenomena of ourselves resp. of our self-processes become accessible to us, namely that we are physical, social, teleological and intentional actors, and that we constantly meet something of the world resp. that something befalls us and generates resp. changes stirrings and impulses of us. Insofar we _are_ our body resp. our bodily processes. On the other hand, we experience as actors as well as because of certain befalling more and more that we have certain corporal compartments, hands, arms, legs, feet etc., which we individually and passively sense and may actively use resp. even must use, to perform certain activities. By this we more and more find out that we _have_ a corpus, which we appropriate that way, which we conceive as something belonging to us, and the features of which can be investigated by natural sciences, features, which are partly general, partly specific, partly individually belonging to us. By this, bodiliness and corporeity have some effect on other things and beings and on ourselves. Bodiliness, corporeity and effectivity thus are fundamental for the occurrence and development of conscious processes. Insofar the main caregivers, in most cases the mother, help infants best in the development of their consciousness by encouraging them again and again to change perspectives, for the perceiving of their bodiliness happens from a totally different perspective, namely from a psychic-motivational one, in comparison with the perceiving of their corporeity, which can happen from a mindful perspective only. But all this we can conceive only, after we have changed our perspective often enough and have experienced our impact from these different perspectives. In the beginning this happens only animated by exchanges with others. Thus, it becomes clear that development of consciousness needs the experience of someone abreast, you meet, as well as your own activity of changing perspectives, of conceiving and of acting.

Considering the five different opposites, which are connected to the five different levels of development of self-consciousness (see chapter 1.2), we see that every opposite first must be overcome to a certain degree, i.e. the opposites must be related with each other up to a certain point, before a change of perspectives may happen and thus the next step of development may be reached. As a physical actor a living being (this is valid for animals and for men) is <u>active</u> by doing something as well as <u>passive</u> by perceiving the results, and only then, when doing and perceiving complement each other and thus are lively related with each other, what happens by desensitization and calming emotions of fascination (as affective impulse), of joy (as sensation) and of fun (as feeling), which bodily stir resp. pulse – desensitization because of frequently repeating the corresponding behavior –, only then it is able to conceive a total impression out of the two perspectives, out of the mindful perspective of active doing and out of the materialistic perspective of the passive let-oneself-befall resp. let-oneself-getting-seized. The more doing and conceiving are related with each other in a living manner, the more immediate gets the total impression, which in the beginning maybe was only conceptualized. By this impression, the living being in concern realizes more and more that it cannot always succeed in doing some specific activity. This way it can handle the corresponding circumstances and can gradually <u>regard</u> (here already the <u>social</u> arises), by what such activities become possible. Here physiological-corporal processes play an important role, because if an excitement does not decrease, a living being cannot process anything, especially change between two perspectives, and therefore does not learn to conceive specified requirements as such. From the neurobiology, we know about the physiological corpus that an excitement of the amygdaline that is too strong triggers a blockade in the hippocampus and thus hinders a further processing in the cortical structures, i.e. without dealing and calming the emotions, there will be no building up a social self, comprehending when-then-rules.

As a social actor a living being is <u>subjectively</u> concentrated on itself as an actor and on its stirrings and impulses, but thereby the same way attentive towards the <u>objective</u> circumstances and activities of others, and only, when the regarding of others and the concentration on oneself, namely objective phenomena seen from a materialistic perspective and subjective phenomena seen from a psychic one, are lively related with each other more and more and thus more and more become an immediate total impression, and when at the same time it deals with its bodily impulses of some affective flare, of some sense of anger and of some feelings of rage, it is able to build <u>teleological</u> chains of activities, by which the next act can be done under the regard of the result of the previous act. Since here we must deal with the calming of an emotional excitement, too, the same physiological-corporal explanation as in the former paragraph hits the point.

If on the level of the teleological self, when a <u>discontinuous</u> breakup of a chain of activities happens, because there was an unexpected result of a previous activity or something unforeseeable happened hindering the next activity of the chain, this fact becomes the condition for the <u>continuous</u> concatenation of another next activity, the corresponding living being can consequently pursue <u>intentions</u> because of this flexibility. But this flexibility develops only then, discontinuity seen from a partly materialistic perspective (something unforeseeable happens), partly mindful one (an unexpected result) and continuity seen from a partly mindful perspective (planned protection against possible eventualities), partly psychic one (trust in one´s own planning) convey more and more an immediate total impression only then, when the bodily stirrings and impulses of an affective shock, of a sensation of anxiety, and of a feeling of fear can be calmed. Since here we must deal with the calming of an emotional excitement, too, the same physiological-corporal explanation as in the former paragraphs hits the point.

Let us now come to the level of the intentional self: to straight reach one´s intentions or to try again and again, until one´s intentions are fulfilled, meaning to get forward in a <u>linear</u> or <u>circular</u> way, these are related with each other in a living manner only then, when the living being in concern can deal with its bodily stirrings and impulses, being affectively painfully touched, sensing grief, or feeling desperate suffering because of not getting something it wishes for itself most yearningly. Animals, e.g. primates, give up at this point distinctly earlier than human beings, so that they cannot reach the next step of evolution resp. the next developmental level. Men have a substantial bigger endurance only, because they share their intentions, their despair, and their suffering and can empathize with each other and see the situation from the perspective of somebody else. Only because of this, they develop the typical human self-consciousness on the level of the <u>representational</u> self, because they can console each other, what calms their physical-corporal excitement, and then they begin to question their intentions, and by this their affects, sensations and feelings resp. their psychic perspective as well as their general sight, their individual judgments and their logical conclusions resp. their mindful perspective. These two perspectives are lively related with each other more and more, so that they are acting more and more in a responsible-reflected manner. At first somebody else questions my perspective, after he had consoled me to make me able to understand, and then finally I begin for myself to question myself as well. By qualifying my intentions, the opposites of a linear pursuing of my qualified intentions, which seems to be ideal from a mindful perspective, and a circular one, when I feel urged to try again and again from a psychic-motivational perspective, will be lively related with each other and thus convey more and more an immediate understanding resp. an immediate total impression, and the way itself, be it linear or circular, becomes the actual goal, i.e. my intention more and more becomes the intention to develop – this remains the claim of mindfulness – while preserving a harmony as best as possible – and this the psychic claim. In contrast to all animals, the opposite between the psychic-motivational perspective resp. the psychic aspect of our being-there and the mindful-idealistic perspective resp. the mindful aspect becomes explicit for us human beings, and thus able to be consciously perceived. We can handle this opposite in a responsible manner and try to overcome it, and by this we would have been arriving at the state of perfect loving.

By questioning our emotions and our thinking, and by investigating and researching our stirrings, impulses, and thoughts, we human beings conceptualize opposites and polarize, i.e. by the opposites active-passive, objective-subjective, continuous-discontinuous and linear-circular, which we already partly had related with each other in a living manner, in the process of our bodiliness by calming, in the process of our corporality by learning to adopt new perspectives, and altogether in the self-process as shown above to be able to understand more and more immediately. By these concepts, which may help us to be oriented mindfully, the next opposite spatial-temporal arises, a combination of all the previous four: someone, who actively, subjectively only coming from himself, by leaps and bounds taking all possible opportunities (discontinuously) and straight pursues his intentions and thus has a mindful perspective, such a person wants to succeed as fast as possible, approvingly accepting to take the space of everybody else, i.e. for him only time is important, and the common space is rather indifferent, while another person, who at first passively perceiving, objectively regarding the circumstances, taking care for continuity and patiently waiting (circular) seeks to fulfill her intentions, by this has a psychic perspective, does not bother about her time and gives space to others, i.e. for her the common space is very important and time is rather indifferent. Moreover, when we are spatially oriented more and more exactly, e.g. where which rules of living together are valid, our temporal orientation diminishes, when which behavior is appropriate, and vice versa our spatial orientation decreases, the more exactly we plan temporally.

Interesting in this context is that in German language and grammar mind and space are masculine and psyche and time are feminine. This demonstrates, at least in our culture, the relation of male and female: for the psyche (female) space (male) is important and for the mind (male) time (female), and from any tension between mind and psyche, male and female, grows the opposite spatial-temporal. As described in chapter 2.2, all opposites would disappear, if there was not any tension between the (relative) psychic-motivational processes, which we verbally express on the level of a denoting-apophantic communication (here even chimps can communicate), and the (absolute) mindful-idealistic processes, which we speak symbolic-hermeneutically of (impossible for animals). This would be possible if and only if all the psychic and the mindful perspectives would convey an immediate total impression to me, which all the materialistic perspectives would be included in as well, since each one of these is conveyed by some psychic and some mindful perspective. This total impression would be true resp. genuine, too, because if not, there would be some delusion, which I could perceive from some perspective that would not be included in my total impression, a contradiction. Since my total impression would be true and immediate, I would truly and immediately understand the for-the-sake-of-which of everyone I meet and of myself. This would be perfect love as I have defined it in "Dasein, um zu lieben" (Kolb, 2017a). If and only if we could understand us in the for-the-sake-of-which truly and immediately, thus if and only if our psychic perspective of the immediate bodily sensing would be in perfect unity with the mindful perspective of realizing without delusion, namely if and only if in perfect love, each opposite as such would disappear.

Because I related human thinking with speaking and language (Kolb, 2017e, p. 57 et seqq., 4th chapter), I would like to go more in the details of these phenomena and of the phenomenon of the two different levels of language (symbolic-hermeneutic and denoting-apophantic), which we meet the first time in early childhood, when three years old infants are able to change between the two modes of experiencing, the as-if-mode and the equivalence-mode (Fonagy, Gergely, Jurist, & Target, 2004). Then e.g. they have learnt, how to use the word "ghost". Wittgenstein means, we speak of a ghost, _as if_ something exists, but for what there is no available _equivalent_ thing. "Where by our language, we suppose a body, and there is no body, there, we would like to say, will be a ghost." (own translation of: „Wo unsere Sprache uns einen Körper vermuten lässt, und kein Körper ist, dort, möchten wir sagen, sei ein Geist." (§ 36, Wittgenstein, 2001)).

If suffering from ghost or phantom pain, to take another example, psychically I am in the equivalence-mode and sense my state as equivalent to the state before amputation. Eventually I make myself dependent from others, may be from a doctor, who tells me, I could not hurt, though I am suffering. Perhaps I am quite aghast and believe the doctor and not myself, as if my sensations and my thinking about it are false and therefore not my sensations proper and my thinking proper, as if my psyche and my mind are not my own psyche and my own mind, as if I first must be ensouled and inspired from outside, and up to now I am only a zombie, whom you can make nearly everything with, whom you may use at will. My corpus, which now I "objectively" perceive as an object, and which I am no more subjectively as my body, will be so to say ensouled and equipped with some mind, a sort of ensouling and inspiring from outside, and me, I am only a corpus, only dust, nothing, determined from outside and not by myself. Me, as a self, in this imagination is my corpus, and my soul resp. psyche and my mind resp. my spirit, these are not belonging to me – and this is schizophrenic.

"Inside" and "outside" here are used in the sense that "inside" means belonging to oneself, and "outside" denotes something different, which does not belong to oneself. Staemmler criticizes the usage of these concepts and that of internalization (Staemmler, 2015, p. 96 - 101). To this I must add that usually we denote with "inside", what we accept as belonging to us, and where we persuade ourselves that it belongs to us alone, and often additionally, as if we could have it at command. Accordingly, "outside" mostly means something, which is unfamiliar for us, what we often do not accept as well, and where we persuade ourselves that we had nothing to do with it. But the more our ability to love gets near to a utopian perfectness and our consciousness widens more and more, the more dislimn the borders of "inside" and "outside", and in the utopia of perfect love this contrariety would be nullified like all other ones.

When imagining the ensoulment and inspiring from outside, only then I am not schizophrenic, I myself am still my soul resp. psyche and my spirit resp. mind, if I become aware that from experiencing, I _am_ my sensations and in the equivalence-mode, and I can change into the as-if-mode. In this mode, I _have_ feelings, which are related to corresponding imaginations, which I _have_ then. This is quite normal and necessary, in order that I can decide, which alternative of my capability-to-be I want to or should accomplish by acting and which one I do or should not. In the as-if-mode I mindfully imagine these alternatives. With different imaginations, there are linked different feelings, so that I get different feelings, when I appropriate different imaginations, e.g. some conveyed by others. In this sense, there may take place an inspiring and ensoulment from outside.

If I express the argument and the emotion of somebody else und believe, it is my argument and my emotion, though this is incorrect, then I am in the equivalence-mode and at the same moment in an abnormal state of consciousness, e.g. in hypnosis or in a psychotic exacerbation. In the as-if-mode however, I am like somebody, who is playing the role of somebody else and knows about it. Then I know as well that my corporal expression is hiding my true self. We say mostly that our corpus (we say body, but mean corpus) as an object proposes an obstacle for others to recognize my soul and my mind. In a psychotic exacerbation, my corpus is this for me myself, too. Then I talk like being in the as-if-mode, even though I am in the equivalence-mode, namely that I take my mindful imaginations (as-if-mode) for equivalent with reality, so that both modes are mixed.

By contrast Wittgenstein means that the "human body [...] is the best picture of the human soul" (Wittgenstein, 2001, p. 1002, PU 496, own translation). In this sense body (I think, Wittgenstein means by human body that, what I denote as body here) and soul are equivalent, and exactly this is meant by the equivalence-mode of experiencing. When our body is the best picture of our soul, then I trust in that I am understandable in my utterances for others, who perceive me bodily. My soul has become bodily in this sense, has representationally become flesh outwardly, an incarnation to the outside and thus conceivable for others, and my body is the fleshly picture of my soul. My corpus sometime later will crumble into dust, but by death my body simply stops to exist resp. to expose itself (the literal translation of the Latin word "exsistere"). As my body, I am the fleshly image of my soul and thus understandable resp. evident for myself as well, once I can mirror myself in others, see myself with their empathic eyes, I am self-evidently my body.

If now I perceive myself as my body, then I say, I am me myself, I am my body. A literal self-evident being-my-body, if it shall not be schizophrenic like the imagination of an ensoulment and inspiring from outside as mentioned above, however, this presumes that I identify not only my self-process, but also my soul resp. psyche and my mind with my body, but is this not schizophrenic? It is evident that the self (always as a process!) is phenomenally contained in our seizedness and our expectations and thus in our psyche resp. soul and our mind, and it is derivable from our delusions and thus from our body with its corporal ownness (I want to denote the total phenomenon of body and corpus as corporal body) – more exactly expressed, from the bodily-material aspect of our being-there (Kolb, 2017a). Derivable, because our body is the best picture of our soul, and because our corporal features partly are the result of mindful developments (e.g. because I want to get a certain appearance, I am starving, doing exercise or have an operation), and phenomenally contained, because our self is grasped by the world and is expecting fulfilment, and if I no more expect any fulfillment and therefore are not seized by the world, this is only the deficient mode of my expectantly being seized. Thus, if I identify my self with my corporal body, this is the same, as if I would say to my picture in a mirror: "Oh, that´s me!" If this would be literally true, then I had doubled, and this really would be schizophrenic. But since normally in everyday-life I am going to say to my mirror image that it is me without believing to be doubled, then I also may say that self-evidently I am my corporal body with its corporal ownness without putting my self as identic to it, i.e. without being schizophrenic. Thus, when I say, "I am my body", I am in an equivalence-mode of experiencing, because my self and my body, both as processes, are on the one hand equivalent, but on the other hand not the same. When imagining becoming flesh outwardly, I indeed view my corporal body as an image and do not put it just as the same with my self that is only represented by it. The aspects of psyche and mind have come into the world by becoming fleshly in a corporal body, have come into reality, so that I can perceive their impact on the world. From experiencing you may call this equivalence-mode, also because psyche and mind have become flesh in our corporal bodies, have become relative and equivalent to it, and can, may, shall, must prove themselves as (relative) representations of our (relational) being-there in dealing with reality in our practical life. By this practicing I am in the reality mode of experiencing.

At first sight, both imaginations of the ensoulment and inspiring from outside and the becoming fleshly outwardly seem to contradict themselves, but if we regard the development of children in the mother-child-relationship of the first years, both takes place in parallel. On the one hand the mother inspires her children from outside, and the children are in the as-if-mode of experiencing, and while in contact with her they appropriate different imaginations during the process of communication by corresponding thinking, and they are ensouled by their mother from outside, when she e.g. is empathically touching them, the children then being in the equivalence-mode of experiencing, because they are experiencing the love of their mother at their body, which is equivalent to their soul. On the other hand, by experiencing, the children are dealing with the world in both modes, and their soul develops in the equivalence-mode and their mind in the as-if-mode, and both processes become more and more visible in the "flesh" of their corporal body and its expression, and thus more and more equivalent to their corporal body, until at the end of this part of development after about four years the children start to connect both modes and likewise mind and psyche more and more. A model for this is, how their mother combines her inspiring and ensoulment of her children. Moreover, the relationship with their father gains the special meaning that he brings the experiencing in the reality mode near to the children in an alternative way compared with their mother. From this point of time this is very useful, because the children combine both other modes, which together indeed convey the reality mode.

The love between mother and child is developing in a similar way like later in other relationships of the child resp. the later grown-up: At first both perceive each other as her child, she has born, and as her or his mother, whom he or she recognizes by her voice, she or he has heard in the uterus, or by the taste of his or her mother's milk which tastes like the amniotic fluid, and both get to know each other and their particular peculiarities more and more – later on, there are may be pheromones, a certain look or certain behaviors, i.e. certain peculiarities, which convey certain kinds of relationships to others. What here takes place in the mode of genus, has distinct relations to the bodily aspect, but also to the psychic-motivational one, because experiencing bodily processes happens in the equivalence mode and thus influences the sensational states of mind and the sensations, and this leads to certain mindful imaginations in the mode of the individual, which you will experience in the as-if-mode. These influence your activities in the mode of the species, the consequences of which make real the equivalence as well as the as-if, so that your experiencing takes place in a reality mode which either confirms the equivalence and the as-if or reveals one of them or both as delusions. These in some circumstances new insights then shape the relationship more and more, so that the love and the ability to love can go on developing more and more. As you easily may see, the three modes of experiencing, equivalence-mode, as-if-mode and reality mode, are in an absolute dialectical relationship like the three modes of being-there, the mode of the genus, of the individual, and of the species resp. the three aspects of being-there of the psychic-motivational (equivalence), the mindful-idealistic (as-if) and the bodily-material (reality). In the mode of individuum the children as objects of the psychic-motivational aspect are in the equivalence-mode of experiencing and as mindful subjects in the as-if-mode, and the better they can combine both being-there aspects and modes of experiencing, the more developed is their individuality, their holistic self-understanding, and their personality (definition see footnote 4 on page 28).

The development of love in a partnership then runs this way: At the beginning, you are lovestruck, and believe to recognize your ideal match in the other. But as time goes by, the as-if-imaginations do not get fulfilled, and the seizedness, equivalent to the lovestruckness, becomes frustrated, so that it comes to a crisis of the relationship. This bigger and bigger unfolding of this seizedness and of the ideal imagination of the other threatens to become more and more chaotic, so that this affords more harmony in form of commitments (dedicating future possibilities) and tolerance (less and less taking something personally evil), both being acts of love (see 2.2, p. 28). Then the relationship again gets more harmonic by not only demanding something ideal from the other, but also by developing oneself and his or her own ability to love further. If this is working out, whereby some-times it is important to support each other, but also sometimes to leave each other alone, then the love between both is developing more and more, until it reaches a niveau that all their disagreements and controversies cannot touch it anymore.

In the beginning of their mindful development children start to "have" a corpus in their imaginations of the possibilities of their ability to be, a corpus that they may use, but in the run of their development, when these imaginations become more and more differentiated, they identify themselves with their different parts of their corpus and "are" their body more and more. Seen from the psychic-motivational aspect they "are" at first their body only, sense themselves as part of their mother, until they perceive little by little that they "have" different corporal realms and thus altogether a corpus different from their mothers´. Correspondingly, the psychic-motivational aspect first is related to the past only, which the children would like to re-gain, if it was fulfilling, and only bit by bit they will be attracted by ideal future possibilities because of their sensations; and seen from the mindful-idealistic aspect, in the beginning the children are oriented to an imagined future, which they have seen fulfilled for others, and incorporates only step by step previous own possibilities into their imaginations. Thus, soul and mind get more and more connected, but always maintain a certain independence, which would be abolished in perfect love only.

The ensoulment and inspiring from outside (in the beginning by the mother usually) is the "joint lock of the outside world" (in German "Hebel der Außenwelt"), as E.T.A. Hoffmann writes, which awakens the "desire of love" (in German "Sehnsucht der Liebe"), as it says in Schopenhauer´s metaphysic of gender love (in German "Metaphysik der Geschlechterliebe"), the lever that moves those forces, which lead to what you may call becoming fleshly outwardly. For us sometimes this seems to be like a carnival (carne means flesh, valere to be worth or valid), if the "flesh" is insisting on worth and validity, sometimes in a grotesque manner, and is demanding its rights. Then the world from the standpoint of mindfulness – in the as-if-mode – seems to be upside down, and our being-there is getting delusional traits like in Shakespeare's Midsummer Night's Dream. In this case laughing resp. humor may create a sound distance and dissolve the delusion.

During adolescence juveniles are learning to hide their psyche resp. sensations and their thoughts resp. mind behind their sexually developing corporal body more and more, until as grown-ups they show themselves with their sensations and thoughts corporally and bodily in an intimate bodily relationship again more and more. Like this it may go to and fro that once the corpus hides psyche and mind, and then again, the body reveals both. We may here recognize some rhythm of development of our human being-there, which does not develop linearly towards the utopian goal of perfect love, but partly linearly, partly circularly.

But psyche and mind are never perfectly united, this would only be the case in perfect love. Because of this, as-if-mode and equivalence-mode are connected, but despite this, are different. The same is valid for the both levels of language, which we use on the one hand in the as-if-mode to talk about the transcendental resp. the absolute and say that we, as an absolute and inaccessible self, have a corpus, and on the other hand in the equivalence-mode to speak of the relative resp. of the secularistic phenomena, when we must say that in our relative being-there we are our body. If we confuse this and e.g. mix having a corpus or being our body, then we confuse absolute and relative, and this is delusional/psychotic. Because superstition is the same sort of confusion, there we find delusional traits, too (Kolb, 2017d). By the acting contact with our environment we can dissolve this and experience in the reality mode, what possibilities we really have with our corpus and in which way we really are our body with its impulses.

Let us come back to the phenomenon of phantom pain. Here, there is most of all a psychic problem. If psychically, where we only later discover the as-if-mode and the future possibilities, we do not yet understand that we only have possibilities to sense something in one leg, then occasionally we sense phantom pain, since psychically we are geared to the painful past, when our leg had to be amputated because of pain and illness (it is known that phantom pain comes up even more and worse, the bigger the pain was before amputation). So, our psyche summons our mind to care for our leg. After an amputation, our psyche must conceive that we <u>no</u> longer <u>are</u> a body with an aching leg. Our mind does not yet conceive the equivalence-mode and past conditions, when we <u>were</u> a body with an aching leg. If now we would listen to our psyche, because we understand mindfully to deal with the as-if-mode and the possibility, <u>as if</u> we still would have two legs, and if we would stand up and try to walk with two legs, we would fall down and from our mind would understand rather quickly by this delusion and disappointment that we no longer have available the possibility of this ability to be, and that we <u>have</u> one leg only.

Quite in general, we best understand something by positively given facts we can perceive, grasp and conceive. A delusion you may perceive, and so this is such a positively given fact. But not to be a body with an aching leg despite earlier extremely painful experiences and sensations with such a body, this is a negative fact, so that from our psyche it is essentially more difficult to conceive this fact of a non-pain. Insofar the phantom pain first is a psychic problem.

The more we understand the equivalence-mode and thus the psychic-motivational aspect by our mind and so, in the as-if-mode, can create an enactment, in which we bodily sense ourselves with undamaged legs, what e.g. may be worked out by a method of mirroring (the existing leg gets mirrored, in the mirror it looks, <u>as if</u> it would be the amputated one, and gets bodily identified with this (<u>equivalence</u>), so that touching the existing leg at the points, where there is the phantom pain of the other leg, conveys the impression at the leg existing only in the mirror that in <u>reality</u> there is nothing aching any more, but another positively given stimulus), the more we conceive from the psychic aspect that our body is rid of our phantom pain, and mind and psyche conceive and understand the same.

In the end, you can trace back all psychic problems to that there is a preceding experience, which like a phantom emerges again and again and influences our emotions in a way that earlier or later we are confronted with unsolvable problems, if we cannot stop this influence. A psychic problem we always have then, when from the psychic-motivational aspect we want to avoid or achieve something, but when we because of past experiences are affectively unpleasantly touched, are negatively set by sensations, and so, tuned by feelings, fear that we cannot do or achieve, or cannot do or achieve without disadvantage, what we want. By the phantom pain, it is the preceding experience not to gain control of the pain. Only when this experience has become more and more meaningless by more and more other experiences, the psychic problem is solved. With the phantom pain, this may succeed with the mirror-method as described above, by conveying the impression that the amputated leg does no longer hurt, but one experiences another tactile stimulus as real. With other psychic problems it may help to newly enact certain key scenes, which have conveyed the corresponding experience, by sort of a psychodrama or trance phantasy, or you can at once act out parts of the self-process, in which the problem occurs, thus working it through, because in the end by dealing with psychic problems the point is always this self-process, which is influenced by the mirroring of others, but which we also can change by our own reflecting (as-if-mode), identifying (equivalence-mode) and experiencing (reality mode).

For such a change, the identifying must take place in the equivalence-mode, since we must deal with psychic problems, and the experiencing in the reality mode. Seen from the psychic-motivational aspect we are indeed our body, so that all changes must be gone through bodily and corporal. Using the mirror-method for solving the problem of the phantom pain, the person in charge indeed experiences bodily and corporal by the touch of the same place, where he or she means to sense the pain at the amputated leg, at the existing leg that at the reflection, which she or he identifies with the amputated leg, nothing hurts anymore.

So altogether three things are important and decisive for solving psychic problems: (1) the own mindful reflecting the psychic problem in the as-if-mode, to create a vehicle for experiencing, and (2) the bodily identifying in the equivalence-mode, and (3) the bodily experiencing in the reality mode. To work with key scenes, where usually important caregivers play their roll, normally means to work with the desire and the avoidance for a different treatment of one´s own self, e.g. to be seen more or to be seen in a different way. Like with phantom pain, mirroring one´s self-process (by setting in scene) and after a bodily perceptible identification of the critical point putting one´s fingers on this, so that one can grasp and conceive that there is no problem anymore, may help to solve the psychic problem. The self-process is indeed (1) dialogical (mode of the <u>genus</u>) in the quasi <u>rhythmically</u> turn taking interplay of different positions (and this dialogue you can enact again and again), (2) abstracting (mode of the <u>individual</u>) in the <u>temporally</u> growing self-understanding (by this anew enacting), and (3) acting (mode of the <u>species</u>) in the <u>spatially</u> engaging dealing with the world (because after the changed enacting you can engage anew).

In the psychotherapeutic situation a patient often unconsciously transfers a certain role to the therapist and thus in the as-if-mode creates a vehicle for his or her experiencing. Then, by identifying with the corresponding complementary role in the equivalence-mode, she or he has the possibility to process her or his psychic problem in the reality-mode, when the therapist facilitates her or him an alternative experiencing by a different mirroring. To consolidate the ensemble, both can make themselves realize this process.

The example of the phantom pain, which you can transfer to all psychic problems, shows the limits of the psychic and the bodily aspect, but if we break down our body into corporal details and view them as a corpus we have, this shows the limits of the mindful aspect, which tarnishes the view of the whole. It is the same as if we had a broken mirror, we only see a distorted picture, the corpus as a broken-up body is an obstacle to recognize psyche and mind, especially our sensations. There are e.g. medical findings, where each doctor means that the corresponding man must have strong pain, but this is not the case, and there are others, who suffer e.g. from back pain, and no doctor can find anything. This way the psychic-mindful may be concealed for others. If we e.g. break down our body by misusing it (chronic exhaustion or substance abuse), we risk besides medical damage (a broken-up body) so called psychic and mental deceases either. Then the psychic-mindful is concealed for us, too.

Generally, you may say that by the development of consciousness there is again and again building up a tension between the psychic-motivational and the mindful-idealistic aspect, namely between seizedness and expectation, which in the material field you may recognize as delusion. On the one hand, we have a corpus seen from our mind, which we want to deploy, use and often misuse for our ideals, on the other hand by our psyche we are a body with needs and sometimes phantom needs wanting to be satisfied. "Grub first, then ethics [resp. ideals]" (in German „Erst kommt das Fressen, dann kommt die Moral"), that way Bertolt Brecht expressed this problem in his "Dreigroschenoper", where he is caricaturing both, as if we would be on the one hand still wild beasts and on the other hand naïve moralists or cagey consummate hypocrites.

4. Being-There-Analytic Explanation of Psychic Disturbances

On the one hand, at this point, it is about the concept of psychic disturbances (the concept of psychic problems has been mentioned at the end of chapter 3.6), on the other hand about their ontological meaning, both seen from the perspective of my being-there analysis each.

4.1. The Concept of Psychic Disturbances

Psychic disturbance I shall call each longer lasting problem of the relationship of being-there to its being-in-the-world, which either directly is involved with the psychic-motivational aspect of being-there or is influenced by that. Such a disturbance of being-there is directly involved with the psychic aspect, if as psychic subject it is about to conceive something it has perceived, or if as object of psyche it must bear and tolerate its sensations. Such disturbances arise from psychic problems as described at the end of chapter 3.6. Influenced by the psychic is such a disturbance, if being-there as mindful subjects we are confronted with the task to consider and plan possibilities, how to bear and tolerate our sensations better, and if as objects of mind we see ourselves confronted with the mission of accomplishing our plans and if as material subjects we want to implement this as skillfully and artistically as possible. Not concerned by the psychic-motivational aspect in our being-there we only are as objects of matter, if we are restricted in our perceptive capability because of corporal circumstances, and as material subject, if we correspondingly are corporally disabled concerning certain abilities and capabilities, and if we accept the fact that these perceptional as well as action-like abilities and capabilities cannot principally be bettered by learning and/or realizing.

The better, however, being-there we can conceive such restrictions of our abilities and bear and tolerate our corresponding sensations better and better, the less they disturb the relation between being-there and our being-in-the-world, and in the ideal case, they constitute no disturbance whatsoever. That psychic disturbances as disturbances of the relationship between being-there and being-in-the-world always disturb the development of the capability to love of being-there, is clear, because this developmental task is the performance-gestalt of the entire living form of being-there and thus of the entire relationship between being-there and being-in-the-world (see 2.2). Because of the previous considerations the reverse is valid as well, namely that all longer lasting disturbances of the development of the capability to love of being-there always contain psychic disturbances. The psychic-motivational aspect indeed is the dynamic one of perfect love (ibidem), and with the development always the dynamic is disturbed as well.

Obviously not every psychic interference is requiring treatment, only then, when being-there you permanently do not get along with it in your environment any more. Over time a corresponding big degree of suffering arises, which seen from the ontological viewpoint develops from that the being-there, which principally suffers from being separated from perfect love as its performance-gestalt, does experience no relief, because there is no more progress of its capability to love. All such progress makes life, namely the relationship between being-there and being-in-the-world, a little easier, since one's origin becomes more and more meaningless, there are more and more future possibilities one has given up (because of decisions) and the situation, in which being-there one has arrived, is accepted more and more gratefully. But if it comes to a stop of this development, the meaningful happenings, which being-there one comes from, accumulate more and more, are less and less processed and thus strain the relationship between being-there and being-in-the-world – one's life – more and more.

Let us now come to the different possibilities to gather and categorize psychic disturbances: this may happen e.g. by that you locate them on the circle of wise and responsible acting (see

2.3), where they disturb the process, which brings us nearer to the goal of perfect love. It is the process, where (1) in the mode of genus we affectively better and better conceive the perceived matters and for what we need others, in the beginning of our life even very intensively, further where (2) in the mode of individuum we sensationally understand the conceived matters (3) to implement the sensationally understood matters in the mode of species expectantly feeling and to perceive resp. receive the result of the action. This result then gets affectively conceived again in this endless process etc. After having gathered all possible psychic disturbances that way, we can categorize them correspondingly:

If somebody in the mode of genus conceives the perceived matters more and more poorly, he or she either may slide into a delusional imagination and thus into a psychotic episode putting the blame on persons or parts of the environment, or if realizing her or his own deficiencies and that his or her affective conceiving has been inadequate, then she or he may either sidestep forward on the circle of responsible action and develop an obsessional rumination as mindful subject or recede on this circle and repeat certain actions as material subject more and more often, so that from that an obsessional control arises.

If somebody in the mode of individuum hardly understands the conceived matters sensationally and thus does not find a possibility of her or his capability-to-be, she or he either may slide into an addiction (substantial or non-substantial) sedating his or her sensations by this and putting the blame on persons or parts of the environment, or if realizing her or his own deficiencies and that his or her sensational understanding does not function correctly, then she or he may either sidestep forward on the circle of responsible action and develop a mixture of actionism and apathy or recede on this circle and as psychic subject remain clinging to an idée fixe with his affective conceiving. (One has ascertained that alcoholics getting abstinent averagely show more evidence for psychotic disorders in the MMPI than before their abstinence.)

If somebody in the mode of species cannot correctly implement her or his decisions or does not dare, he or she either may slide into a depression putting the blame on persons or parts of the environment, or if realizing her or his own deficiencies and that his or her decisions or lack of self-confidence are inadequate, then she or he may either sidestep forward on the circle of responsible action and invent more or less weak excuses as psychic subject or recede on this circle and develop unfeasible plans as mindful subject, so that others often interpret this neurotic behavior as stupidity or laziness.

A special form of psychic disturbances appears, if somebody interprets the information resp. the results of her or his actions always that way, that he or she never can be called to account or be responsible. This disturbance sometimes appears like a psychotic episode, like an addiction or a strong anxious-depressive neurosis, however, it is neither the one nor the other, but a borderline syndrome.

Using this categorization of psychic disturbances, the following phenomenal basics become evident:

1. You can distinguish psychic disturbances by, *in which mode* they have their origin, whereby as a rule the ones in the mode of *genus* are the most difficult and the most serious ones, then come the ones in the mode of *individuum*, and finally the ones in the mode of *species*.

2. You can distinguish psychic disturbances by, whether the being-there realizes its deficiencies and deals with it as a *subject*, or if it perseveres as an *object* and deems others or its environment deficient. The latter normally introduces bigger problems for the treatment.

3. If the being-there gets active as a subject, there is the distinction, if it sidesteps forward on the circle of the wise and responsible action or recedes backward, in both cases away from its difficulties. The corresponding active *strategy of processing*, as you may call this going forward or receding, can be even more complex as mentioned in the previous examples, because the being-there may go on further forward or backward, and if it never stops, then probably, there exists a borderline syndrome –

when constantly going forward the "common" borderline personality disorder, when constantly receding the narcissistic borderline syndrome (the idée fixe thereby is the narcistic hubris).

These assemblies and categorizations do not assert a claim of completeness and certainly still can be refined essentially, but in the end, I only wanted to demonstrate exemplarily, how this scheme of responsible human acting, by means of which the different mechanisms of suppression could be described, too (see 2.3), can be used for gathering and classification of psychic disturbances.

4.2. Sense and Meaning of Psychic Disturbances

To find out sense and meaning of something, namely to understand it, you need a frame resp. a framework of sense, a structure (Latin structura may be translated by framework of sense) or preferably several structures, by means of which you can analyze and interpret psychic disturbances in this case. Here the being-there structures timeliness, spatiality, and reality of life offer themselves for this purpose, or the structure of processuality with its four ecstasies of origin, future, arrival, and information. The first three ecstasies together constitute the timeliness, the fourth one the spatiality, and because of the absolute dialectical relationship of the three being-there structures of timeliness, spatiality, and reality of life, the four ecstasies of processuality convey the reality of life. Just as the sense of being, the sense of psychic disturbances is understandable in the frame of these four ecstasies.

If the primordial disturbance has occurred in the mode of genus and somebody inadequately affectively conceives or has conceived something perceived (from the past) on the concrete-ontic level, so that delusions come from that, then on the ontological level – ontological means intrinsically underlying and giving sense – she or he as being-there is at odds with his or her fate or thrownness, senses anger as intrinsic sensation because of the information given about her or his origin. This existencial[12] anger hinders the further development, since the anger gives so much weight to the origin that the concrete past existence cannot be released and sink into meaninglessness. The communication with others, who do not cling to the past like this, is disturbed more and more, and thus no communicative solidarity can develop, contrarily, being-there one gets more and more distrustful or even hostile and senses one's situation as one of overextension. But instead of bearing the intrinsic anger, being-there one first and foremost falls back on non-intrinsic ways of being, meaning one changes the mode of one's emotions from sensation to feeling (in terms of Heidegger from intrinsic to non-intrinsic – I shall use both terminologies), gets rage on, grief because of someone or something concrete, or fears something threatening.

If the primordial disturbance has occurred in the mode of individuum and on the concrete-ontic level somebody inadequately or not at all does sensationally understand, in any case does not find any acceptable possibility of his or her capability-to-be or only such ones that experientially lead to delusions, then on the ontological level he or she senses anxiety as intrinsic sensation because of the information given about her or his future, namely that he or she is responsible for it, and that inevitably he or she will come to the end of life, her or him facing a sure but indeterminate end. By this existencial anxiety the future of the relationship between being-there and being-in-the-world, meaning all possibilities of her or his capability-to-be, gets such an appeal that these concrete possibilities cannot be given up any more, decisions become more and more difficult, a holistic self-understanding can be developed less and less, contrarily, an inadequate pride develops or an inadequate inferiority complex leading to further and further self-delusions, so that being-there one

---

[12] "Existential" refers to all existing things, "existencial" only to human beings according to Heidegger, who replaced categories by "Existenziale", if humans are meant. With "existencial" I want to denote everything that relates to Heidegger's "Existenziale". Since the representations we create of ourselves can change our human being-there, categories are inadequate for being-there. To accept an interpretation of myself may be the first step that I shall change myself.

senses one's situation as one of helplessness. Here, however, being-there one can fall back on choosing a lesser evil, namely some non-intrinsic ways to be (see above).

Finally, if the primordial disturbance has occurred in the mode of species and on the concrete-ontic level somebody inadequately does not understand practically to energetically implement the chosen possibilities of his or her capability-to-be, so that the expectations according to her or his feeling do not get fulfilled, then on the ontological level he or she senses suffering as intrinsic sensation because of the information given about her or his situation, where he or she has been arrived, namely him or her hopelessly being and remaining separated from her or his intrinsic self, meaning from perfect love. By this existencial suffering from being separated from perfect love any kind of autonomy and effectiveness vanishes, being-there one senses oneself as sport of some forces no matter which, and senses one's situation as one of hopelessness. Here, again, being-there one can fall back on choosing a lesser evil, namely instead of suffering from being separated either non-intrinsic grief because of concrete losses, non-intrinsic fear of threats or of concrete responsibility (the pressure of which may seem worse than death, so that death can be viewed as release and brought to pass by suicide), or non-intrinsic rage on previous concrete happenings seen as damages.

If the primordial disturbance comes from that on the concrete-ontic level the being-there trusts or accepts no information about one's deficiencies, meaning the denial of one's capability-to-be-guilty as with a borderline syndrome (the central psycho-therapeutic intervention in the treatment of this disturbance is to confront the patients with honest feedback of others teaching them to trust and accept the information about what they elicit from others), then one gets submerged by fear of or rage on something concrete as feelings each, meaning ontologically by anxiety of accepting responsibility for being-there (containing the anxiety of being-towards-the-end) and the anger about the beginning of being, namely its thrownness, both anxiety and anger as intrinsic sensations, so that he or she dissociates and backtracks, until she or he concrete-ontically cannot stand his or her feeling of loneliness resp. ontologically that she or he is separated from his or her intrinsic self, from perfect love, and thus seeks for company with the concrete world resp. with somebody. Thus, it can go to and fro, and the spatiality as the ontic-concrete opposite of proximity and distance as well as the dynamic of the sensations described above, because she or he does not trust the information about his or her relationship between being-there and being-in-the-world, these determine the problems of being-there, for the individual information as spatial ecstasy burdens the being-there with these sensations. This pattern of proximity and distance is a typical pattern of relationship of the borderline syndrome. Because of the disturbed ecstasy of information (ontological) resp. because of the disturbed pattern of relationship (ontic) neither a mature superego formation nor the ability to sublime (see 3.5) will develop.

This analysis shows us that not alone the sensation of anxiety of taking responsibility for one's being-there and the one of death as being-towards-the-end, which being-there one is ontologically confronted with, but also the anger of thrownness and the suffering of being separated from one's intrinsic self resp. from perfect love are at least unbearable the same way. This mates that during the infantile development, where the degree of difficulty of the situation to be coped with increases more and more, infants first feel rage because of a situation of overextension, then fear of a situation of helplessness, and finally grief because of a situation of hopelessness, i.e. the intrinsic resp. individual sensation of anger seems to be bearable the easiest way, then comes anxiety, and the most difficult seems to be to deal with the sensation of suffering. Thus, defense or acceptance of suffering plays an important role when developing one's ability to love. The Islamic mystic Rumi has written: "Don't look for water, but become thirsty", i.e. "don't fend off your suffering, but accept and bear it to know what you need". The importance of suffering before any other sensation the medieval mystic Master Eckart also stresses when saying "Suffering is the fastest steed to God". Correspondingly, it says in the Tibetan Buddhism that it is the easiest way to get out of the Wheel of Rebirth, if you are in the human state or realm sensing your own suffering and that one of others.

By intrinsic suffering, it is not meant any kind of psychic pain, but a sensation, which basically and profoundly underlies our being-human, namely "such one, what for one thing and most commonly is *not* showing itself, what is *concealed* in contrast to that, what is showing first and foremost, but at the same time is something that belongs to that showing first and foremost, in fact that way that it represents its sense and reason" (Heidegger, Sein und Zeit, 2006a, p. 35, own translation), and this is the desire for perfect love, as well as the intrinsic anger of being separated from it and the intrinsic anxiety, never to find back again. With the aid of our intrinsic sensation of suffering we can pierce through sense and reason of our being (freely cited according to Master Eckart), and thus advance to the absolute nothingness (according to Buddhism) resp. to perfect love more and more. Just as well, however, we can pierce through certain obstacles by our intrinsic anger or by our intrinsic anxiety.

When Freud introduced the death drive into the theory of psychoanalysis 1920 in "Jenseits des Lustprinzips" (Freud, 1975), a drive, with which he linked not only the regression – according to Heidegger the bringing-back to the beginning of being-there – but also the aggression, where one wants to destroy one´s life, then this can be interpreted in my opinion that he brought in the intrinsic anger about the thrownness of being-there from its beginning into his theoretical view. Thrownness means that the being-there has been separated from perfect love by being thrown into the world, and because of this anger one wants to go back before one´s existence in this world, and no existence means death. Together with the intrinsic anxiety of taking responsibility for one´s being-there and the one of the end of being-there, by which the being-there decisively runs forward to its end and must face up to the possibility never reaching perfect love, the entire relationship between being-there and being-in-the-world (the whole life) is encompassed, and this altogether conveys the desire for its intrinsic self resp. for perfect love, for its intrinsic being and for its intrinsic not-being uniting both life drive and death drive.

The anxiety of being-towards-the-end means that it is even now critical for the being-there to ever reach perfect love.

The desire implies the intrinsic sensation of suffering because of being separated from perfect love. This suffering mediates between anger and anxiety and is conveyed by both. Correspondingly you can show that anger mediates between anxiety and suffering, and both convey this anger, as well as anxiety mediating between anger and suffering, both conveying this anxiety. Between the intrinsic anger, the intrinsic anxiety, and the intrinsic suffering thus, there is an absolute dialectical conveying relationship, so that none of these intrinsic sensations can be preferred. With the aid of all three sensations again and again we can pierce through sense and reason of being-there and thus progress on our way to the absolute nothingness resp. to perfect love, for concerning all three intrinsic sensations it is about perfect love.

If the intrinsic anger because of one's thrownness that being-there one has been separated from perfect love, gets too strong, then being-there one normally looks for possibilities to ease one's sensation, i.e. one converts the anger into a feeling of rage about something concrete and tries to change the concerning concrete and negative factor (a disadvantage, a damage or the like). This will be accomplished only to a certain degree, until being-there one comes to a border earlier or later, where one alternates between actionism and lethargy thus trying to cope with the situation (in psychoanalytic terms). Then one can be released from one's efforts, which in some cases may have the character of overextension, only by that with the aid of one's intrinsic anxiety or one's intrinsic suffering one pierces through the bottom of one's soul, and that it appears to one that all striving will have a secure end or that the overextension is because one is separated from one's true self and is too little able to love. Therefore, in both cases excessive efforts are senseless. This works until being-there one gets overwhelmed by one's intrinsic anxiety of taking responsibility for one's being-there and the one of being-towards-the-end that possibly one will never reach perfect love, or correspondingly overwhelmed by one's intrinsic suffering to be hopelessly separated from one's true self resp. from perfect love.

If one cannot bear one's intrinsic anxiety, then being-there one normally looks for possibilities to ease one's sensation, i.e. being-there one converts the anxiety into a feeling of fear of something concrete and tries to fend off the concerning concrete threat. This will be accomplished only to a certain degree, until being-there one comes to a border earlier or later, where one may flee into an addiction, defending (in psychoanalytic terms) one's emotions. Then one can be released from one's helplessness only by that with the aid of one's intrinsic suffering or one's intrinsic anger one pierces through the bottom of one's soul, and that it appears to one that indeed being-there one is separated from one's true self resp. from perfect love just now in this moment or has been separated earlier. If one was or had not been separated, then one could deal with all threats and even with death. Again, this works only, until one gets overwhelmed by one's intrinsic suffering or anger.

If one cannot bear one's intrinsic suffering, then being-there one normally looks for possibilities to ease one's sensation, i.e. one converts the suffering into a feeling of grief of something concrete and tries to overcome the concerning concrete separation. This will be accomplished only to a certain degree, until being-there one comes to a border earlier or later, where one finally separates oneself (in psychoanalytic terms) from the situation. Then one can be released from one's hopelessness only by that with the aid of one's intrinsic anger or one's intrinsic anxiety one pierces through the bottom of one's soul, and that it appears to one that one had built up an ideal image and had chased after a phantom image, which had fooled one and drawn a red herring across one's track. This works, until being-there one gets again overwhelmed by one's intrinsic anger about one's thrownness and thus being separated from perfect love or by one's intrinsic anxiety that had shown that the real danger had been veiled by the wrong ideal.

The last three sections have shown sense and meaning of suppression as this term is used in psychoanalysis with the three forms of coping, defense, and separation, and this showed some possibilities, which could more and more lead to release: The awareness (1) of one's death resp. one's being-towards-the-end and one's responsibility for one's being-there connected with the anxiety possibly never to reach perfect love, (2) of one's inauthenticity resp. deficiencies connected with the suffering being

separated from perfect love, and (3) of one´s thrownness into il-
lusions and delusions connected with the anger that being-there
one had been separated from perfect love anyway – each of these
pierces through the bottom of one´s soul of being-there and thus
leads to the absolute nothingness resp. to perfect love.

5. Psychotherapeutic Consequences

In common with the psychic disturbances it applies to psychotherapy as well to consider two layers, namely the layer of the concrete-ontic measures in the psychotherapeutic setting and the ontological layer, where it is about, what is essentially at the basis of it and provides it with sense and reason.

At first for this I want to look at the role and meaning of the one to be treated, who is called in one case patient and in another client, meaning once a suffering one (from Latin pati = to tolerate, to suffer, to forbear, to acquiesce) and once a follower, a devotee, a dependent one (from Latin cliens = fellow, servant, attendant, ward). Up next it is about the role and meaning of the psychotherapist, who at least seen from the word meaning shall seek to get some opening of the soul (from Greek psyche = soul, thera = chase, seeking, and peuthô = indication, information, opening). Finally, the relationship between both plays a role and has some meaning, too, because here two human beings meet, who in each case on one side are absolutely for themselves and independent, but on the other side relative and dependent from the other one (Nishitani, 2011).

5.1. Patient or Client

Both concepts have both adequate and misleading meanings from Latin in my opinion: on the one hand, "patient" as somebody suffering is indeed adequate, because if she or he did not suffer, he or she would not come to psychotherapy, and she or he who comes without suffering, is out of place. On the other hand, "patient" as somebody passively tolerating is misleading, since suffering ones wanting to undergo a psychotherapy not always are passively tolerating. However, as you could see in 4.1, their suffering comes from that they have turned away from themselves and can only solve this by that they decisively strive after information as true and immediate as possible about origin, future, and/or arrival of their situation. So, they need to be resp.

to become an active and decisively seeking subject, they may not remain forbearing ones in this sense. Concerning effective solutions, everybody suffering from psychic disturbances is passive and should be activated in the right direction.

The concept of the client as a ward is adequate on the one hand, because this one as somebody suffering needs protection as a start to calm down a little bit, because she or he who is too excited cannot process anything, any information is useless and therefore no information for him or her, so that all her or his efforts cannot lead to anything. On the other hand, the meaning of client as follower, servant, and attendant suggests that he or she does not act autonomously resp. self-responsible, but only according to instructions of superiors. Insofar both concepts are partly appropriate, partly not, so that I decide for the concept of patient, because it better reveals the meaning of suffering (see 4.2) and emphasizes the importance of an adequate activation.

The role of the patient must be or become one of an active subject acting self-responsible and not submitting to any instructions. Further she or he should keep open for any information (1) as object of matter concerning her or his affects and delusions, (2) as object of psyche regarding his or her sensations and seizedness resp. consternation, and (3) as object of mind what her or his feelings or expectations reveal.

Ontologically, meaning what underlies our being essentially, this role of patients means that they keep ready for all their intrinsic sensations, (1) for their anger about their thrownness, meaning that they have been separated from perfect love, (2) for their anxiety to assume the responsibility for their being-there, and for their being-towards-the-end, for their definite, but temporarily and by circumstances uncertain very own death as the possible end of all their hopes to reach perfect love, and (3) for their suffering because of their momentary being separated from their authentic being and not-being, from the utopia of perfect love.

How and by what can patients manage to adopt the role described above? Which aids can a psychotherapist make available to them for that? Since patients themselves shall become active subjects, the therapist must not restrict them by rules, she or he must quasi give them anti-rules. Alice Holzhey-Kunz, by interpreting the Freudian rule that patients shall totally unrestrictedly associate and uncompromisingly report everything that first crosses their mind, as such an anti-rule (Holzhey-Kunz, 2014, p. 198), and by reasoning this by that patients should keep open for the existencial anxiety quite according to Heidegger, she shows, how the psychoanalytic setting can make the patient an active subject. Another example for an anti-rule you find in gestalt therapy, when Fritz Perls tells his patient: "Make a void and let nature fill in!" By such anti-rules, patients get guided to face up to the opposite active-passive, to deal better and better with it, and finally by this to overcome it better and better. This opposite they have met for the first time on the developmental level of the physical self, and by anti-rules they get to know the sense and the nonsense of rules.

In the face of death, of one´s responsibility for being-there, of one´s thrownness, and one´s being separated, being-there one is always confronted with the aspect of the unavailability of one´s being-there. Getting invited to be subject, patients are earlier or later confronted with this objective aspect, and by that the therapist does not help them, the patients are prompted to bear this, i.e. they are prompted to see that again and again they are objects as well, and thus they get the opportunity to overcome the opposite subjective-objective better and better, which they have met the first time on the developmental level of the social self, and so they get to know the sense and the nonsense of different kinds of weltanschauung.

When the therapist again and again calls the patients´ attention to their sensational states of mind, she or he also highlights the aspect of the unavailability of being-there. Insofar mirroring the emotional contents of utterances of patients like in client-centered therapy is supporting them, for many aspects of emotions are unavailable when being there, especially all affects. With bodily sensations it is the same, because of which hypnotherapeutic treatments, which focus the patients upon psychic and bodily sensations most of all without influencing any processing, can be psychotherapeutically very useful. Freud has refused hypnosis in his days I suppose, because in its form at that time when using it therapeutically hypnotherapists have guided their patients too rigid and made them an object.

When such processes – elicited by freely associating thoughts, by the free development of sensational states of mind, and by freely observing bodily sensations, each of which shows the unavailability of the three being-there aspects mind, psyche, and body – are highlighted, patients more and more can discover, how continuously, but also how disjointedly, and how straight, but also circularly these processes can proceed, so that more and more they can overcome the opposites continuous-discontinuous and linear-circular, which they have met the first time on the developmental levels of the teleological and the intentional self, and so they get to know the sense and the nonsense of both skillfulness and purposefulness.

By all this, patients again and again are assessing the events and their experiences as good or bad, and ideally, they realize more and more clearly, how relative are such value judgements. In a certain context something seems to be positive, but in another negative, and this may change to and fro depending on the spatial perspective or on time. Thus, the relativity of space and time resp. the opposite special-temporal gets clearer and clearer to them, which they have met the first time on the developmental level of the representational self, and so they get to know the sense and the nonsense of value judgements, moral and ethics.

The following story from Taoism may demonstrate, what I mean by this: In former times and in a place, where you still could find something like wilderness, the only horse of a peasant run away, so that he did not know how to till his field. Full of empathy the people of his village said: "Too bad!", but he only shrugged his shoulders and said: "Good or bad, who knows?" Some days later the eloped horse came back from wilderness, and three wild horses followed. "What good luck!", people said, but the peasant only shrugged his shoulders and said: "Good or bad, who knows?" Again, some days later the peasant´s son tried to tame one of the wild horses and to ride it but was pitched and broke his leg. "Too bad!", the people cried, but the peasant only shrugged his shoulders and said: "Good or bad, who knows?"

Shortly afterwards heralds of the king came, who wanted to go to war, and all young men of the village had to come with them except for one. "What good luck!", the people cried, but the peasant only shrugged his shoulders and said: "Good or bad, who knows?" This story you could tell on and on, and it would remain always insecure, what should be valued how.

If thus with the help of the therapist patients get on and on overcoming all these described opposites, they more and more reach the utopian state of perfect love (Kolb, 2017a, p. 135 et seqq., chapter 3.8).

Altogether, the role of the patients is sufficiently described, and too, how the therapist can support them. At this point I want to plead in favor of combining different therapeutic treatments, for not each patient is open and able at any time to use one or another assistance of the therapist. Sometimes e.g. freely associating helps better, but sometimes to focus upon one's sensational state of mind, one's breathing, one's bodily posture or bodily sensations.

5.2. The Role and Attitude of a Psychotherapist

The role of the psychotherapists is chiefly confined to support patients in their role, to call their attention to opposites, and to convey them the aspect of the unavailability of being-there. Since on the ontological layer, where you only can understand this aspect, their own unavailability is covered for the patients first and foremost and they discover this by other ones first, as already Heidegger remarked (Heidegger, 2006a), it may be very helpful, if the therapist shows her or his own unavailability to the patients, e.g. by not fulfilling certain expectations of them.

Further, it is important for therapists clearly to differentiate when to assume a supporting role in terms of clearing the way, and when a confronting one, to make obvious, which responsibility every man must bear. Here, for me it is valid that nobody is responsible for the actual life-situation one is thrown in, but for that however, how one deals with it, namely if and how one lets oneself in for it. If somebody gets into it decisively, therapists should intervene supporting as best as they can, and if one does not let oneself in a bit, they should confront this behavior. Since most of the patients partly get into it and partly not, it is most convenient to react positively when they let themselves in for it supporting them in this. Often, they get themselves more and more into it, and only that points, which they avoid even after considerable time, you should question (preferably by I-messages like: "I wonder why …") and thus confront this.

Concretely, it is about in each case that the psychotherapist when intervening keeps the patients by the flow of their free associations, by their different emerging psychic and/or bodily sensations. Maybe depending on the situation, they change between the different aspects of mind, psyche, and matter, meaning associations, sensational states of mind, and bodily sensations, and thus between different perspectives, whereby a big skittishness of patients should be observed and registered. If this flow falters or again and again starts over and by a change does not come forward resp. gets started, it may be helpful, if under these circumstances the therapist incorporates his or her own free associations, sensational states of mind or bodily sensations. By this she or he demonstrates the patients his or her own unavailability. So, patients can recognize the therapists' unavailability and finally their own one. In this sense demonstrating the therapists' unavailability is a seeking for opening the soul (Greek: thera peuthô), patients get so to say open-minded resp. more and more open-minded, so that the free flow of their utterances of their thoughts, sensational states of mind or bodily sensations can go on flowing. Altogether for all of them including the therapist, the ecstasy of information becomes important, because only this can convey the opening.

On the one hand the therapist achieving this task must keep open for the actual and intrinsic sensational states of mind of the patients by

1. that he or she, paying attention to the ecstasy of *origin*, is listening to the individual history of her or his patients, which may be covered behind their symptoms, their rela-

tional offerings towards the therapist, and every other utterance of the patients, and thus, paying attention to the ecstasy of *information*, is open for their intrinsic anger about their thrownness that they have been separated from perfect love,

2. that he or she, paying attention to the ecstasy of *future*, is listening to the general expectations and concerns of her or his patients, which also may be covered behind their symptoms, their relational offerings towards the therapist, and every other utterance of the patients, and thus, paying attention to the ecstasy of *information*, is open for their intrinsic anxiety about their being prompted to assume responsibility for their being-there and for their unsurpassable being-towards-the-end, when all hopes have ended to be able to reach perfect love,

3. and that he or she, paying attention to the ecstasy of *arrival*, is listening to the specific actual wishes and aspirations of her or his patients, which, as it is with the ecstasies of origin and future, may be covered behind their symptoms, their relational offerings towards the therapist, and every other utterance of the patients, and thus, paying attention to the ecstasy of *information*, is open for their intrinsic suffering because of their actual being-separated from their authentic self, meaning from perfect love.

To be able to show her or his own unavailability, *on the other hand* therapists must keep open for their own intrinsic sensational states of mind of anger about their thrownness, of anxiety about assuming responsibility for being-there and being-towards-the-end of all hopes, and of suffering because of their being separated from their authentic being and not-being resp. from perfect love. For this attitude, too, there can be no rule, but only non- or anti-rules, just as Holzhey-Kunz interprets the Freudian rule of listening by evenly suspended attention (Holzhey-Kunz, 2014, p. 198). The rule for patients (see 5.1) recommended by

Fritz Perls may be endorsed to therapists as well, and when Milton Erickson, the so-called father of modern hypnotherapy, tells about himself that when confronted by a difficult patient he himself goes into trance, then all these recommendations and anti-rules are geared towards the same attitude of therapists.

By this attitude psychotherapists listen to, what appears within the horizons of origin, future, and arrival both concerning patients and themselves – this still is quite concrete-ontic – and additionally they pay attention, what comes along within the horizon of information, namely "such one, what for one thing and most commonly is *not* showing itself, what is *concealed* in contrast to that, what is showing first and foremost, but at the same time is something that belongs to that showing first and foremost, in fact that way that it represents its sense and reason" (Heidegger, 2006a, p. 35, own translation). This once more shows the special importance of the ecstasy of information, which the ontological-intrinsic can be made accessible by, which is concealed behind that, what appears within the horizon of the three temporal ecstasies.

When the therapist utters thoughts first coming into mind in free association, after she or he has realized that the flow of his or her patient is faltering or starting over again and again, then you may view this as interpretation the therapist construes about her or his patient. Because the therapist's attitude is the same as the one she or he recommends or has recommended to his or her patients, the patients are not restricted or even dominated, but contrarily actually supported in their role as patients, because this clears the way for further spontaneous utterances of them about their thoughts, emotions, and bodily sensations, i.e. the therapist remains true to her or his aims and his or her role. At this point we already have reached the therapeutic relationship.

5.3. The Relation between Patient and Therapist

As just now shown patient and therapist encounter themselves as coequal persons setting themselves the same task and correspondingly bestir themselves, namely to keep open in their intrinsic sensational states of mind of anger, anxiety, and suffering. Insofar both are ontologically-intrinsically absolutely independent, what is concretely-ontically shown by e.g. that each of them totally independently from each other can finish the psychotherapeutic relation. At the same time and coincidently with this absolute independence both are ontologically-intrinsically absolutely dependent from each other, what is concretely-ontically becoming clear e.g. that the therapist can be no therapist, if the patient does not admit it, and that vice versa the patient can be no patient, if the therapist does not yield to this arrangement. The absolute dependence you can also describe this way that both are *subject* to each other, each of whom can affectively conceive and sensationally understand the other one's for-the-sake-of-which and can autonomously act towards the other one. Both are each *for/pro* the other one, as Paul Sartre expressed it (Sartre, 1993).

This opposite dependent-independent underlies every relationship and thus each relational problem, too. A relationship and thus a psychotherapeutic one resp. the entire psychotherapeutic treatment can succeed if and only if this opposite is overcome again and again. Nishitani describes this as the opposite of freedom and equality (Nishitani, 2011). What intrinsically-ontologically underlies each concrete-ontic solution, he allegorically describes by the following story: Two Zen-masters, who know each other by names only, meet the first time personally. Master A then asks Master B for his name, and this one answers: "I am master A." Thereupon master A exclaims: "But this is me! Who are you?" At that master B answers: "I am master B.", and both are laughing.

Applied to the psychotherapeutic situation and relation the following appears: After patients have started with the free flow of utterances of associations, sensational states of mind, and/or bodily sensations, earlier or later they will begin to falter, because concretely-ontically e.g. the whole issue is too silly for them, the silence of the therapist gets eerie to them, or they want to please the therapist. What this ontologically-intrinsically underlies, is the intrinsic anger ("too silly") about the thrownness onto the momentary situation, the intrinsic anxiety about the eeriness of being-in-the-world, one had to assume responsibility for, and what may be finished at any time, or the intrinsic suffering because of being separated from one's authentic self resp. from perfect love, what one projects upon the therapist by wanting to please her or him. Here on the ontological layer patient and therapist meet the first time, and by pausing the patient asks the therapist for her or his for-the-sake-of-which (this is the meaning of the name in the Zen-story). The therapist, by reacting to the faltering of her or his patients this way that he or she undertakes their role and assumes and continues the flow of their utterances, she or he answers: "I am the patient" or "I am you". If the utterances of the therapist fit the free flow of the patients' utterances and continue them, then patients state resp. it gets open to them, even if they still do not correctly discover it: "Indeed, this is me!", and the more they discover that, the more they will concretely-ontically get full of rage or fearful about that the therapist has read their character and seems to know them better than they themselves, or full of grief because they are so far away and separated from their intrinsic capabilities and dexteries they discover that the therapist has them. Here as well, we again can recognize the three intrinsic sensational states of mind of anger, anxiety, and suffering on the ontological layer. When this ideally gains more and more space for the patients and they better and better become moved or move themselves into the ecstasy of information, they will finally ask the therapist quite openly, who she or he is, and by putting him- or herself as far as possible into the ecstasy of information showing her- or himself in his or her being-there, the tension is solved, and both can laugh enjoying their relationship, so that healing may begin.

For this whole process it is important that therapist and patient do not stick on any concepts, especially that they release all their concepts of power and do not try to dominate, to exploit, and to manipulate each other. If the Freudian rule of listening by evenly suspended attention is conceived that way as anti-rule, then it complements the other two anti-rules mentioned in 5.1

and 5.2 perfectly. You may describe this process of mutual releasing by this as well: If the therapists forget they are therapists and the patients they are patients, then healing may start.

5.4. Interpretations of the Therapist and the Goal of Therapy

To sum up, you may state at this point that by a psychotherapy the intermediate goals of the therapist should be on the one hand a regulation of the excitement of her or his patients and on the other hand a suggestion, encouragement, and exhortation for them to change perspectives again and again in order to capture as many aspects of being-there as possible. To achieve this the interpretation of the therapist plays an important role, and it should serve the superior goal of the development of the capability to love, which is the gestalt of performance for the whole human life determining our entire "Lebensform", meaning the total relational form between being-there and being-in-the-world we indeed are all about.

Concerning the interpretation of the therapist according to the previous considerations you may formulate that the therapist indirectly tells the patient: "I am you." By this however, he or she does not help in a deputizing-dominating manner, but in a projecting-liberating one, as Heidegger expressed it (Heidegger, 2006a), by fortifying and encouraging her or his patients to freely let flow further the utterances about their mental associations, sensational states of mind, and bodily sensations, and to overcome corresponding obstacles, which ontologically-essentially the intrinsic anger about their thrownness underlie, and the intrinsic anxiety about assuming their past, future, and present both being and not-being, and the intrinsic suffering because of their being separated from their authentic self, i.e. from perfect love. Thereby, the unawareness of the patients plays a big role, a state, the nature of which it is that we keep ourselves in suspense by not being able or not wanting to compare, because we do not process certain emotional contents of our memory, i.e. do not integrate them in our biographic memory.

Here an example from my own practical work: A patient, who rather often had complained of the relationship with her husband and had considered again and again, if she should part company with him, had begun a still tentative affair with another man. One day during a therapy session she particularized me, how this friend had maltreated her. Thereby in her thoughts, it only pivoted on the incidents, how he would have hurt her. After a while I spontaneously uttered: "But then you still can stay with your husband." Thereupon she laughed, and soon she could release the issue of her injury. Later near the end of our therapy, she explained to me that this was one of the turning points in her therapy, and that this utterance on my part would accompany her up to now. Since I myself have not been aware of this meaning and effect of my intervention (I had not compared this incident with others and so not recognized its meaning for my patient), I was wondering, what this whole thing could make clear to myself.

On the one hand, it came home to me once more, what a big importance humor has in all interhuman encounters – my patient had been laughing after my remark, the two Zen-masters at the end of the story above, too. Among pedagogues there is a saying that a lesson, where not at least once they were laughing, is no good lesson. In my opinion this may be applied to therapy sessions as well. Humor is quasi an ideal way to initiate a perspectival change by bringing things into a new context.

On the other hand, I for myself associated thoughts about this utterance, which had slipped out of my mouth in this therapy session so spontaneously, and finally came to the topic "To remain with oneself", another formulation of Freud's rule of the therapist's abstinence. When commenting the situation of my patient, I was on one side authentic and thus perfectly with myself, on the other side I had burst out and concerning this not been remaining with myself. I had been remaining with myself by not remaining with myself. My demonstration of overcoming this opposite, what I did not realize at all, made my patient solving her conflict, whether she should stay with her husband or not, by remaining with herself looking for and finding solution approaches of her matrimonial problems together with her husband. Insofar with my remark I had on the one hand assumed her point of view

("I am you"), on the other hand, however, I had removed an obstacle of thinking and thus cleared the way for her to work on her actual and essential difficulties to remain with herself and to love herself.

My intervention first had finished her unawareness by comparing both relationships with her friend and her husband. Subsequently in the therapeutic situation she switched from the mindful subject in the mode of individuum, namely as she was busy with the possibilities only, how best to treat her friend, to the mode of species as material subject by talking about her relationship with her husband, and finally to the one of genus and conceived as psychic subject, how much she was addicted to a sort of love delusion. Beyond the therapeutic situation she switched from a compensatory way of acting out as material subject in the mode of species, namely as she continuously met her friend making and feeling rather dependent from him, to the mode of genus by exchanging views with her husband, and then to the one of individuum by considering and as mindful subject planning possibilities of solving their matrimonial difficulties, and finally as material subject in the mode of species she autonomously and successfully came to grips with her husband. Ontologically-intrinsically she had pierced through the bottom of her soul, which seemed to consist of suffering only, with the aid of her intrinsic anger about her thrownness to be separated from perfect love (concretely, to be alienated from her husband and exposed to the relationship with this friend).

This "I am you" of the Zen-story is to discover the hidden, essential obstacles and to make patients understand that and eventually exemplarily how they can overcome them. Concerning the revealing this is a real interpretation, and regarding the making-conceivable it works inviting and liberating, so that it is real protreptic (from Greek Protreptikos, an encouraging and admonishing scripture by Aristotle to be concerned with philosophy). This is also suitable for the therapeutic goal formulated by Holzhey-Kunz, to make patients, suffering from their being-there-like clairaudience, human beings being philosophically experienced (Holzhey-Kunz, 2014, p. 263).

While other psychotherapeutic interpretations, especially the psychoanalytic one, stay on the concrete-ontic level, the being-there analysis deals with the concealed problems of being-there, thus revealing quite different coherences, which necessarily never can be perfectly unveiled, and which always relate to momentary phenomena. Therapist and patient thereby are encouraged to open for the ontic-ontological difference. Concretely, the therapist can invite patients to open that way by that she or he points delusions out to them, under which they are either as psychic subject when conceiving (e.g. when they are too strongly seized by certain proceedings) or as mindful subject when sensationally understanding (e.g. when they have got too strongly positive or negative expectations when planning certain projects) or as material subjects when practically understanding and performing plans (e.g. when they demand too high or too low standards of themselves concerning their capabilities and dexterities when performing certain plans). After patients have conceived each of these, the therapist may ask them, whether they therefore hold themselves in suspense about their delusions (this is unawareness, see p. 90, chapter 3.5), meaning that they are avoiding a true information about it, because they are angry about their being-in-the-world, or anxious for that, or suffering from that, and that as a consequence they also evade any information about that they sense this anger, this anxiety, or this suffering. By this namely, they prevent that emotional contents get integrated in the biographic memory.

These intrinsic sensational states of mind of anger, anxiety, and suffering in general are very contradictory: on the one hand we are ontologically-essentially angry about our thrownness, about that we are expected to put up with something without being asked previously, and then we must manage it, whether we want it or not, we must exist, on the other hand we fear to be taken out of this unreasonably demanded situation anytime by death. On one side we are anxious to assume our existence being responsible for it, on the other side we get angry, if somebody or something wants to seize control from us. We are suffering from our thrownness, from that and how we must live, and we are suffering from that we all must die sometime. Considered that way, you simply cannot please us human beings. The whole issue makes sense only then, if you consider it under the aspect that it is testified by being-there that all men by their essence strive for perfect love, i.e. if you realize that the anger is about that we are separated from perfect love, that we are anxious no more to find back to it, and that we generally are suffering being separated from it. Contradictory it looks only, if you do not include love.

The ambivalence arising by not regarding love then runs through our entire relationship with our being-in-the-world, through our whole life, especially through all interhuman relationships, what is expressed by the following profound cartoon: You see two women, mother and daughter, armed with wooden rolling pins, who, hidden behind the apartment door, are obviously waiting for the husband of the daughter, who probably drunken will come home too late. In this situation one says to the other: "But I hope, he´s OK!" This ambivalence of anger and anxiety, essentially being behind this joke, conveys the painfulness of our existence altogether – I have already shown previously that there is an absolute dialectical relational conveyance between anger, anxiety, and suffering (see 4.2). With all we could be much more joyful, if we could handle our existence like some people manage a visit of other ones, because thereby they are always glad twice, once when they come, and once when they part. Why do we not trust to reach perfect love, resp. why can we not enjoy the same way that once we shall depart this life, like we do to have come into this world, when we e.g. celebrate our birthday?

Certainly, this is a utopian goal like perfect love, and considering more exactly both aims are equivalent. If we would love perfectly, our origin would be meaningless, so we had no anger, we would hand all our future possibilities over, so we were not anxious anymore and altogether were not suffering, too, since anger and anxiety convey suffering, and we would enjoy our existence altogether, especially our thrownness and our mortality. If vice versa we just could enjoy both, we would have neither anger nor anxiety, thus no suffering, and we would hand all our future possibilities over, our origin and thrownness would be meaningless, and we would accept our every-day-life gratefully, altogether we would love perfectly.

Accordingly, it is a reasonable goal, not only for our total relationship with our being-in the-world we indeed are about according to Heidegger (Heidegger, 2006a), but also especially for every psychotherapy, to open our psyche/soul – this is valid for patients as well as for therapists – more and more by developing our capability to love more and more. If in this sense both get something out of it, then actually what get the therapists their fee for? A well-known answer to this question is: The fee for therapists is half and half shush and smart money.

A last, but decisive problem now consists of, how patients – and therapists as well – can be motivated to train their capability to love more and more, what indeed is also exhausting, against the anxiety that it is absolutely impossible to reach perfect love, and that we shall be forever separated from it, so that everything seems painful and futile. On the one hand, the concept of love is rather attractive, and if you can show that freedom, another positive taken concept, closely correlates with love, with this then, we have a strong motivation, at least in our culture. The connection between love and freedom you can show by this: on one side, even Kant has ascertained that you can neither prove nor disprove the existence of human freedom, but that morality based on the categorical imperative makes freedom possible (Kant, 1788). On the other side, it comes from my analysis of being-there and the preconditions I made there that the basic question of ethics is how you can foster the ability of love, and therefore from this the morality of Kant is dependent. Thus, the more freedom is possible, the more you we have developed this ability, and this is the connection between freedom and love. By Donovan this can be heard in his song "Colors" in the last verse, where he is singing: "Freedom is a word that I seldom use without thinking of the time when I´ve been loved."

In a collectivistic society it is more about equality than about freedom, and here it is valid as well that equality is even more perfect, the more developed is the ability to love. Without love resp. without a sufficient understanding, what human beings are seized by, equality can be based on some more or less big coercion, and then equality is not very perfect, since it is instable, and some feel more, and some feel less enforced. With the argument that with the development of our ability to love more and more freedom and equality becomes possible we might motivate all human beings (1) to <u>decide</u> with the corresponding <u>power</u>, (2) to <u>endeavor</u> with the corresponding <u>discipline</u>, and (3) to <u>run the risk of failure</u> with the corresponding <u>courage</u> to improve this ability more and more to understand the for-the-sake-of-which of all to be more and more truly and immediately.

So, what preconditions are necessary, what do we need to promote our ability to love further and further in the direction of perfect love? According to Kant for that we need the reflecting power of judgement (Kant, Critik der Urteilskraft, 1799 (3. Auflage)). In my terminology, thereby it is about the power, the discipline, and the courage (see above) to reflect the circle of prudent thinking and to face up to one´s emotions in a responsible manner, in fact (1) with one´s affects and the corresponding contrasts one has perceived, which can be so stark that one <u>separates</u> them both e.g. after having experienced something traumatic, (2) with one´s sensations and the connected seizedness, which can be sensed so embarrassing that one <u>defends</u> them both, and (3) with one´s feelings and the connected expectations, which can be so bad that one tries to <u>cope</u> with them by actionism or lethargy. These are the three ways of suppression as they are described by the psychoanalytical theory. According to Kant the reflecting power of judgement brings us from a specific experience to general phenomena essentially underlying the whole; in my terms this means from specific situations to the general emotions moving us out of the realm of familiarity (emotion comes from emovere, to move out of) and essentially underlying all incidents, where we meet something strange.

Important tools (see above) are the determination to face up with all phenomena, the endeavoring to learn and exercise new aptitudes and acquirements, and the risk-taking to courageously and responsibly bear and endure the burden of the corresponding sensational state resp. to raise responsible tolerance and courageous openness to others and to oneself (Kolb, 2017c, p. 172 f.). Since we can develop our ability to love never alone – already in our childhood we need significant caregivers, usually our parents – we can master these tools and their usage together with others only. In adulthood marriage resp. a marriage-like partner relationship adopts a particular rank. On the one hand there is the tendency to restore the original unity as it consisted with our mother, on the other hand a relationship two by two is principally more intensive than relationships in a larger community. By the way, both is valid for a therapeutic relationship, but here a developmental incline should exist that therapists have developed their ability to love further and by this exert i. a. a role model function.

On one side therapists should be determined to foster their own ability to love and the one of their patients, on the other side they should have enough self-discipline to solve conflicts encountered again and again – this corresponds to the psychoanalytic requirement of abstinence – and thirdly they should be tolerant and open to all pulses and stirrings of their patients and of themselves – this corresponds to the free-floating attentiveness so called by Freud.

If in a partner relationship there is an incline like in a therapeutic one, then this is no true partner relationship, at least in the beginning, until they reach a certain balance. Thenceforward, it is as well about the determined advancement of the ability to mutually love, about the continual conflict solving with the corresponding self-discipline, and about tolerance and an openness to support each other in some situations, but also to leave each other alone in some other situations

That our striving for perfect love is testified by being-there, and that we can progress on the way to perfect love, and that this may occasionally make our being-there joyful at least for a little time, means nowhere near that our striving will be rewarded sure enough in the end by reaching perfect love. Or must we simply sacrifice this hope once for all? Should this demand, should this claim (is it "The Claim of Reason" (Cavell, 1979)?), become just meaningless for us? Ought we to be simply grateful for the short moments, when we get a faint glimpse of perfect love? Does the advice of Confucius fit here perhaps to convert the way into the goal?

Once liberated
from the big delusion
having looked into
the empty eye of the sphinx,
they forget the earnest
of all earthliness
out of over-earnest,
and they´re only smiling.

(From "The Knowing One" by Christian Morgenstern,
own translation)

Appendix: Being-There Analytical Structures

Since in psychotherapy they more and more focus on the so-called structural disturbances, at this point I want to epitomize the being-there analytical structures used by me. More detailed descriptions or hints, in which books of the list of literature you may find the like of it, are in the main text of this book. Characteristic for my analysis of being-there are

1. the structure of the modalities of being-there genus, individuum, and species combined with
2. the structure of the aspects of being-there psyche, mind, and matter resp. of the psychic-motivational, the mindful-idealistic, and the bodily-material aspect,
3. perceptual structures, namely space, time, and rhythm combined with
4. the structures of being-there spatiality, timeliness, and reality, which correspondingly summon (1) to let oneself in to get along with others in order to get useful information (in German "auskommen", "to get along" and "Auskunft", "information" are related words), (2) to project oneself into the three temporal ecstasies origin, future, and arrival, and (3) to be alive,
5. a memory structure, which distinguishes the emotional memory with the memory of affects, the memory of sensations, and the memory of feelings from the biographic one with the memory of activities and effects, the memory of conditions and concepts, and the memory of possibilities and plans.

In a circular overall structure of all these structures (Kolb, 2017c, p. 235 et seqq., Illustrations and Tables) we can describe various phenomena, which can influence and change the overall and each of its partial structures. Each development comes about by movements on the circle of the overall structure, whereby the movement direction on the circle may change all the time. This emphasizes the unavailability resp. freedom of our being-there with the following three kinds of freedom resp. unavailability: (1) one´s own individual decisional freedom, (2) the specific unavailability of what we meet, and (3) the general freedom of the common exchange with others.

The partial structures 1 to 4 and the one of the emotional and the biographic memory under point 5 have in common that their three elements are in an absolute dialectic relationship, i.e. each one goes between the other ones, and these both convey the first one. By this no element has a precedence over the other ones, and all elements are non-substantial. The prevailing structure being the general aspect, the particular elements being the individual aspect, and the entirety of all interrelations being the specific aspect are in an absolute dialectic relationship as well. In this sense the structure of our being-there is absolute dialectical.

In the beginning the development successively takes place on five hierarchically graduated levels, where the next level is available only when the development on the up to now highest level has reached a certain degree of maturity. At that the development on each achieved level may go on parallel to the one of all other levels, and so never needs to end. The five levels in their order resp. hierarchy are the level of

1. the physical self with the bodily-material anchorage by the opposite active-passive, the psychic-motivational anchorage by the affect of fascination, the sensation of joy, and the feeling of fun, the mindful-idealistic anchorage by the dianoetic virtue of apprehension (conceiving basic principles), and the meaning of language in every-day life of the gustatory sense (to acquire a taste of

something getting active or passively enjoying) – altogether you more and more conceive by this the importance of the ethical principle of diminishing suffer,

2. the social self with the bodily-material anchorage by the opposite subjective-objective, the psychic-motivational anchorage by the affect of flare/reluctance, the sensation of anger/disgust, and the feeling of rage/revulsion, the mindful-idealistic anchorage by the dianoetic virtue of science (if-then-rules), and the meaning of language in everyday life of the olfactory sense (the objective subjectively stinks) – altogether you more and more conceive by this the importance of the ethical principle of fairness,

3. the teleological self with the bodily-material anchorage by the opposite discontinuous-continuous, the psychicmotivational anchorage by the affect of shock, the sensation of anxiety, and the feeling of fear, the mindfulidealistic anchorage by the dianoetic virtue of virtuosity (constructing complex activity chains, i.e. to walk), and the meaning of language in everyday life of the touch sense (to cautiously touch upon something) – altogether you more and more conceive by this the importance of the ethical principle of appropriate hierarchies (you benefit from the skills of somebody higher up in the hierarchy),

4. the intentional self with the bodily-material anchorage by the opposite linear-circular, the psychic-motivational anchorage by the affect of pain, the sensation of suffering, and the feeling of grief, the mindful-idealistic anchorage by the dianoetic virtue of prudence (to gain prudent views to reach one's intentions), and the meaning of language in everyday life of the aural sense (if you won't hear, you must feel, sound of pain) – altogether you more and more conceive by this the importance of

> the ethical principle of loyalty and fidelity by helping each other to reach the purposes of everybody,

5. the representational self with the bodily-material anchorage by the opposite temporal-spatial, the psychic-motivational anchorage by the affect of terror, the sensation of disappointment/shame, and the feeling of indignation, the mindful-idealistic anchorage by the dianoetic virtue of wisdom (acting meaningfully and responsibly), and the meaning of language in everyday life of the visual sense (insight, regard, watchfulness, prospect, circumspect) — altogether you more and more conceive by this the importance of the ethical principle of clean-keeping of social relations (not personally taking evil anything if possible, conceding mistakes, repenting, recompensing if possible and promising to learn from it, also generally giving and keeping promises).

From the puberty on it happens that the sexual self develops with the bodily-material anchorage by the opposite male-female, the psychic-motivational anchorage by the affect of enthusiasm, the sensation of care, and the feeling of passion, the mindful-idealistic anchorage by appreciation, and the meaning of language in everyday life of the commonsense resp. the so called third eye. By this developmental level in the ideal case the previous five ethical principles get consolidated resp. integrated on a common level, because if these principles remain separated, disastrous repetitions of the same aberrations may happen in form of a renunciation of oneself because of exaggerations and/or neglects of certain ethical principles. If you exaggerate the principle of fairness, you may increase suffering, exaggerating the principle of hierarchies may lead to unfair intrigues, when exaggerating the allegiance to certain persons you may forget the merits of others and destroy an appropriate hierarchy, if you accommodate certain people too much to cultivate the relationship, you may make others wary, so that allegiances get weakened. In the worst case all five ethical principles may lose their meaning in the community, so that much suffering will arise, and the development starts from scratch with the ethical principle of diminishing suffering.

With more life-experience a last developmental step may happen, namely the level of the collective self (Kolb, 2017a, p. 149 et seqq., chapter 4), where you more and more recognize worth and sense of life and by that all the more consequently strive for the ultimate goal of a successful life, as Aristotle would have described it, or for the utopian goal of perfect love, as I have called it. This you do then by more and more supporting others concerning their development of their ability to love, and by clearing the way for them. By more and more showing yourself when doing this you more and more overcome the opposite public-private and become more and more conscious of the attachment to all and everything.

During the entire development we more and more conceive the various opposites, i.e. from the angle of the psychic-motivational aspect we more and more get urged to face up to, whether we shall deal with them actively or passively, shall subjectively give priority to ourselves or to objective concerns of the world, whether we shall be mindful of continuity or prefer more variety, whether we shall strive for our goals as linear as possible or stubbornly try again and again, whether we shall give space to ourselves first of all and the world or pay more attention to time settling everything as fast as possible, whether we shall act more according to the so called female principle that we first care for others before we look after our own concerns or according to the so called male principle that we first shall consolidate ourselves before we support others. That way an "opposite-structure" emerges in the psychic-motivational realm resp. in our soul as this is called in the Analytic Psychology of C.G. Jung (Jacobi, 1992, p. 58). At the same time developmentally, it is about the dissolution and overcoming of this opposite-structure resp. of these opposites in dealing with reality. However, this would be completely accomplished in the utopia of perfect love only.

Here now exemplarily, a being-there analytic description of the psychotherapeutically interesting phenomena "self", "I", "person" and their structures as they appear by my being-there analysis: for Heidegger the phenomenon of the self is contained in the concern[13] (Heidegger, 2006a), for me in seizedness, expectation, and delusion[14] (Kolb, 2017a), i.e. the three being-there aspects psyche, mind, and matter open up the view of the self. On the different developmental levels our self gets more and more available and thus recognizable, though not always recognized because sometimes we suppress. Available phenomena only get recognized by a corresponding interest because you must strain yourself to discover them. The self is opposing the phenomenon of the I or the ego, which according to Heidegger often vociferously comes forward (Heidegger, 2006a), which may more and more recognize itself and our self during the course of our development, but which again and again may be wrong, too. Our person is the entire impression of that what, for us or others, "sounds" through the mantle of the entirety of our representations resp. our utterances, so that we or the others think this our self. Thereby delusions are never excluded. In the utopia of perfect love I, person, and self would be the same and completely recognized as our authentic self, "a phenomenon in an excellent sense" (Heidegger, 2006a, p. 35, own translation), namely "such one, what for one thing and most commonly is *not* showing itself, what is *concealed* in contrast to that, what is showing first and foremost [e.g. the phenomenon of the I or ego], but at the same time is something that belongs to that showing first and foremost, in fact that way that it represents its sense and reason" (ibidem,

---

[13] German "Sorge"
[14] German "Ergriffenheit, Erwartung und Täuschung"

own translation). Our authentic self strictly speaking is no phenomenon, it is something absolute, meaning something detached which can never be in our relative world, just as little as perfect love, but we can near both more and more, more and more perfectly love without ever perfectly loving, more and more authenticly be ourselves without ever authenticly be ourselves.

From the angle of the psychic-motivational aspect in the mode of genus self, I, and person in each case appear as a psychic subject with the functions of conceiving and <u>distinguishing</u> conditionalities, whereby it is important to avoid delusions. By this ideally self, I, and person are better and clearer <u>identified</u> concerning each of their conditionalities. From the angle of the same aspect, but in the mode of individuum as object of psyche resp. in the context of a seizedness induced by the identification, the conceived conditionalities get <u>integrated</u>, sometimes also together with phenomena conceived earlier, and self, I, and person are <u>evaluated</u> from the angle of this aspect.

From the angle of the mindful-idealistic aspect in the mode of individuum self, I, and person in each case emerge as a mindful subject with the functions of planning and deciding, whereby it is about to <u>distinguish</u> the different possibilities of being able to be and to <u>identify</u> the best one, so that the expectations built by planning and deciding preferably will not be frustrated and the tensions because of the corresponding seizedness will become <u>regulated</u>. Concerning their theoretic possibilities self, I, and person get identified by this, too. From the same angle, but in the mode of species as object of the mind resp. when practically implementing the decisions, the corresponding possibilities of being able to be resp. the concrete plans get practically <u>evaluated</u> concerning their viability, and thus also self, I, and person in relation to their abilities to plan and to decide.

From the angle if the bodily-material aspect in the mode of species you recognize self, I, and person in each case as bodily subject with the functions of practical acting and executing plans, whereby it is about to <u>distinguish</u> one´s own capabilities and skills and to <u>identify</u> the necessary and preferably appropriate ones and to apply them in an optimal way, in order that the performances and <u>regulations</u> are successful. Concerning this, self, I, and person get identified, too. From the same angle, but in the mode of genus as object of matter resp. when perceiving the progress of acting and finally of the entire result, one´s own capabilities and skills get <u>evaluated</u>. Subsequently the overall context of previous perceiving/distinguishing, conceiving/integrating, and deciding/regulating as well as of seizedness, expectation, and the degree of fulfillment resp. delusion will be identified and evaluated, partly theoretically, partly practically, partly constructing resp. destructing, perhaps together and/or by oneself. This way in each case, an overall image resp. the corresponding identity emerges and an overall evaluation of self, I, and person.

As subject being-there one self-organizes, (1) one distinguishes and dissociates oneself concerning one´s conditionality resp. origin, (2) one determines oneself and decides between different possibilities of being able to be, and (3) when acting one tries for coherent ex- and impression, for consistency in relation to oneself and for continuity in relation to others. However, as object one self-regulates, one tries (1) for communicative solidarity, (2) for a preferably holistic self-understanding of one´s being-there, and (3) for as much as possible autonomy and effectivity when acting, bodily as well as psychic-motivationally (not to be seized by something that is strange to once nature or unattainable) as well as mindfully (no false or fatuous expectations). In perfect love communicative solidarity, holistic self-understanding, and autonomy/effectivity would be absolutely perfect. Dissociation, self-determination, and coherent ex- and impression would be absolutely meaningless.

Literature

Al-Khalili, J., & McFadden, J. (2014). *Life on the Edge.* London: Bantam Press, Imprint of Transworld Publishers.

Arendt, H. (1998). *The Human Condition: Second Edition.* Chicago: The University of Chicago Press.

Aristoteles. (1985). *Philosophische Bibliothek, Bd. 5, Nikomachische Ethik.* (G. Bien, A cura di) Hamburg: Felix Meiner Verlag.

Balint, M. (1988). *Die Urformen der Liebe.* München: dtv/Klett-Cotta.

Cavell, S. (1979). *The Claim of Reason: Wittgenstein, Skepticism, Morality, and Tragedy.* New York: Oxford University Press.

Dreyfus, H., & Taylor, C. (2015). *Retrieving Realism.* Cambridge (Massachusetts): Harvard University Press.

Fonagy, P., Gergely, G., Jurist, E. L., & Target, M. (2004). *Affect Regulation, Mentalization, and the Development of the Self.* New York: Other Press.

Freud, S. (1975). Jenseits des Lustprinzips. In S. Freud, *Studienausgabe, Band III: Psychologie des Unbewussten* (p. 213 - 272). Frankfurt am Main: Fischer.

Hartmann, D. (1998). *Philosophische Grundlagen der Psychologie.* Darmstadt: Wissenschaftliche Buchgesellschaft.

Heidegger, M. (2006a). *Sein und Zeit.* Tübingen: Max Niemeyer Verlag.

Heidegger, M. (2006a). *Sein und Zeit.* Tübingen: Max Niemeyer Verlag.

Heidegger, M. (2006b). *Zollikoner Seminare.* (M. Boss, A cura di) Frankfurt am Main: Vittorio Klostermann GmbH.

Heidegger, M. (2010). *Über den Humanismus.* Frankfurt am Main: Vittorio Klostermann GmbH.

Holzhey-Kunz, A. (2014). *Daseinsanalyse. Der existenzphilosophische Blick auf seelisches Leiden und seine Therapie.* Wien: Facultas Verlags- und Buchhandels AG.

Hoyningen-Huene, P. (1989). *Die Wissenschaftsphilosophie Thomas S. Kuhns.* Braunschweig: Friedrich Vieweg & Sohn Verlagsgesellschaft mbH.

Jacobi, J. (1992). *Die Psychologie von C. G. Jung (1940)*. Frankfurt a. M.: Fischer Taschenbuch Verlag.

Kant, I. (1781 (A), zweite Auflage 1787 (B)). *Critik der reinen Vernunft*. Riga: Johann Friedrich Hartknoch.

Kant, I. (1785 (A), zweite Auflage 1786 (B)). *Grundlegung zur Metaphysik der Sitten*. Riga: Johann Friedrich Hartknoch.

Kant, I. (1788). *Critik der praktischen Vernunft*. Riga: Johann Friedrich Hartknoch.

Kant, I. (1799 (3. Auflage)). *Critik der Urteilskraft*. Berlin: F.T. Lagarde.

Kolb, H.-P. (2011, 01. 10). *Gedanken zu "Sein und Zeit"*. Tratto da Wikiversity, Fachbereich Philosophie: https://de.wikiversity.org/wiki/Gedanken_zu_%22Sein_ und_Zeit%22

Kolb, H.-P. (2012a, 01. 24). *Die Philosophie der Kyôto-Schule*. Tratto da Wikiversity, Fachbereich Philosophie: https://de.wikiversity.org/wiki/Die_Philosophie_der_Ky %C3%B4to-Schule

Kolb, H.-P. (2012b, 06. 27). *Gedanken zu Stanley Cavells "Der Anspruch der Vernunft"*. Tratto da Wikiversity, Fachbereich Philosophie: https://de.wikiversity.org/wiki/Gedanken_zu_Stanley_C avells_%22Der_Anspruch_der_Vernunft%22

Kolb, H.-P. (2017a). *Dasein, um zu lieben. Daseinsanalytische Grundlagen für Psychologie und Psychotherapie (2018 amended version)*. Norderstedt: BoD - Books on Demand.

Kolb, H.-P. (2017b). *Rhythmus, Intuition und Liebe. Die Rolle der Körperlichkeit bei der Daseinsanalyse (2018 amended version)*. Norderstedt: BoD - Books on Demand.

Kolb, H.-P. (2017c). *Liebe, Macht und Sexualität. Wie können wir in diesem Spannungsfeld glücklich werden? (2018 amended version)*. Norderstedt: BoD - Books on Demand.

Kolb, H.-P. (2017d). *Religion, Ökumene und Liebe. Daseinsanalytische Religionsphilosophie (2018 amended version)*. Norderstedt: BoD - Books on Demand.

Kolb, H.-P. (2017e). *Nature and Love. A Teleological Comprehension of Nature (2018 amended version)*. Columbia, SC: Made in USA.

Kolb, H.-P. (2017f). *Liebe und Resonanz. Daseinsanalytische Betrachtungen im Zusammenhang mit Themen der Weltbeziehungen (2018 amended version)*. Norderstedt: BoD - Books on Demand.

McClelland, D. C. (2006). The Harlequin Complex. In R. W. White, *The Study of Lives: Essays on Personality in Honor of Henry A. Murray* (p. 94 - 119). New Brunswick (U.S.A.) and London (U.K.): Aldine Transaction, A Division of Transaction Publishers.

Metzinger, T. (2014). *Der Ego-Tunnel. Eine neue Philosophie des Selbst: Von der Hirnforschung zur Bewusstseinsethik*. München: Piper Verlag GmbH.

Nagel, T. (2012). *Mind and Cosmos: Why The Materialist Neo-Darwinian Conception of Nature is Almost Certainly False*. Oxford: Oxford University Press.

Naumann, B. (A cura di). (2005). *Rhythmus. Spuren eines Wechselspiels in Künsten und Wissenschaften*. Würzburg: Königshausen & Neumann.

Nishida, K. (2011). Selbstidentität und Kontinuität der Welt. In R. Ohashi (Hrsg.), *Die Philosophie der Kyôto-Schule* (E. Weinmayr, Übers., S. 56 - 114). Freiburg im Breisgau: Verlag Karl Alber in der Verlag Herder GmbH.

Nishitani, K. (2011). Vom Wesen der Begegnung. In R. Ohashi (A cura di), *Die Philosophie der Kyôto-Schule* (K. Nishitani, & H. Buchner, Trad., p. 242 - 257). Freiburg im Breisgau: Verlag Karl Alber in der Verlag Herder GmbH.

Ohashi, R. (A cura di). (2011). *Die Philosophie der Kyôto-Schule*. Freiburg im Breisgau: Verlag Karl Alber in der Verlag Herder GmbH.

Rentsch, T. (1999). *Die Konstitution der Moralität: transzendentale Anthropologie und praktische Philosophie*. Frankfurt am Main: Suhrkamp-Taschenbuch Wissenschaft.

Rentsch, T. (A cura di). (2007). *Martin Heidegger – Sein und Zeit*. Berlin: Akademie Verlag GmbH.

Sartre, P. (1993). *Das Sein und das Nichts*. Hamburg: Rowohlt Taschenbuch.

Schmitz, H. (2011). *Der Leib*. Berlin/Boston: de Gruyter.

Staemmler, F.-M. (2015). *Das dialogische Selbst. Postmodernes Menschenbild und psychotherapeutische Praxis.* Stuttgart, Germany: Schattauer GmbH.

Tanabe, H. (2011). Versuch, die Bedeutung der Logik der Spezies zu klären. In R. Ohashi (A cura di), *Die Philosophie der Kyôto-Schule* (J. Laube, Trad., p. 137 - 183). Freiburg im Breisgau: Verlag Karl Alber in der Verlag Herder GmbH.

Ueda, S. (2011). Das absolute Nichts im Zen, bei Eckhart und bei Nietzsche. In R. Ohashi (A cura di), *Die Philosophie der Kyôto-Schule* (S. Thumfart (zweiter und dritter Teil), Trad., p. 440 - 468). Freiburg im Breisgau: Verlag Karl Alber in der Verlag Herder GmbH.

Wittgenstein, L. (2001). *Philosophische Untersuchungen; Kritisch-genetische Edition.* (J. Schulte, A cura di) Frankfurt am Main: Suhrkamp Verlag.

www.ingramcontent.com/pod-product-compliance
Lightning Source LLC
Chambersburg PA
CBHW050817260726
48660CB00004B/1482